THE AUTHOR   Michael Starks studied history at Cambridge and gained first class honours. He now works for the BBC as a manager. A former television producer, he is a keen traveller and student of history. In this, his second book, he brings together these two enthusiasms to enhance holidays in France. He lives in London.

Other Titles in the Series

A Traveller's History of Australia
A Traveller's History of Canada
A Traveller's History of The Caribbean
A Traveller's History of China
A Traveller's History of England
A Traveller's History of France
A Traveller's History of Greece
A Traveller's History of India
A Traveller's History of Ireland
A Traveller's History of Italy
A Traveller's History of Japan
A Traveller's History of London
A Traveller's History of Mexico
A Traveller's History of North Africa
A Traveller's History of Paris
A Traveller's History of Portugal
A Traveller's History of Russia and the USSR
A Traveller's History of Scotland
A Traveller's History of South East Asia
A Traveller's History of Spain
A Traveller's History of Turkey
A Traveller's History of The USA

THE TRAVELLER'S HISTORY SERIES

'Ideal before-you-go reading' *The Daily Telegraph*

'An excellent series of brief histories' *New York Times*

'I want to compliment you ... on the brilliantly concise contents of your books' *Shirley Conran*

Reviews of Individual Titles

A Traveller's History of France

'Undoubtedly the best way to prepare for a trip to France is to bone up on some history. *The Traveller's History of France* by Robert Cole is concise and gives the essential facts in a very readable form.' *The Independent*

A Traveller's History of China

'The author manages to get 2 million years into 300 pages. An excellent addition to a series which is already invaluable, whether you're travelling or not.' *The Guardian*

A Traveller's History of India

'For anyone ... planning a trip to India, the latest in the excellent Traveller's History series ... provides a useful grounding for those whose curiosity exceeds the time available for research.' *The London Evening Standard*

A Traveller's History of Japan

'It succeeds admirably in its goal of making the present country comprehensible through a narrative of its past, with asides on everything from bonsai to *zazen*, in a brisk, highly readable style ... you could easily read it on the flight over, if you skip the movie.' *The Washington Post*

A Traveller's History of Ireland

'For independent, inquisitive travellers traversing the green roads of Ireland, there is no better guide than *A Traveller's History of Ireland*.' *Small Press*

*A Traveller's History of
the Hundred Years War
in France*

To Sue

A Traveller's History of the Hundred Years War in France

MICHAEL STARKS

Interlink Books
An imprint of Interlink Publishing Group, Inc.
New York • Northampton

First American edition published in 2002 by

INTERLINK BOOKS
An imprint of Interlink Publishing Group, Inc.
99 Seventh Avenue • Brooklyn, New York 11215 and
46 Crosby Street • Northampton, Massachusetts 01060
www.interlinkbooks.com

Library of Congress Cataloging-in-Publication Data

Starks, Michael, 1944–
    A traveller's history of the Hundred Years War in France: battlefields, castles, and towns / by Michael Starks.
        p. cm. – (The traveller's history series)
Includes bibliographical references and index.
    ISBN 1-56656-468-9
1. Hundred Years' War, 1339–1453.   2. France–Guidebooks.   3. Historic sites—France—Guidebooks.   I. Title.   II. Traveller's history.
    DC96.5 .S73 2002
    944'.025–dc21

2002004698

Printed and bound in Great Britain

To request a free copy of our 48-page full-color catalog, please call
1-800-238-LINK, visit our web site at **www.interlinkbooks.com**,
or write to us at: **Interlink Publishing**
46 Crosby Street, Northampton, Massachusetts 01060
e-mail: info@interlinkbooks.com

Table of Contents

List of Illustrations

Between pages 116 and 117

Maps and Genealogical Charts

Introduction

This is a holiday history of the Hundred Years War. In other words, it is
the story of that period told in a way that relates to places in France that
travellers can visit. Normandy, Picardy, the Loire and south-west
France are particularly rich in relics and reminders of the medieval
English invasions of France. The guide books tell the story in snippets.
The history books, understandably, have no bias towards the sites that
can help bring the story to life today. So this is a holiday companion, to
be read before and during a visit to France.

The story starts in the fourteenth century, in the reign of Edward III,
the first English king to claim the title of king of France. It ends in 1453,
during the reign of Henry VI, when the claim ceased to have any
credibility, though, remarkably, English monarchs continued to use the
title until the time of Napoleon. It covers Crécy, the Black Death, the
capture of the French king by the Black Prince, the deposition of
Richard II, Agincourt, Joan of Arc, and a period during which the
English actually governed (as distinct from just invaded) substantial parts
of France.

The term 'The Hundred Years War' was only invented in the
nineteenth century. The years between 1337 and 1453 normally
covered by the phrase were not one long war at all, but rather a series
of wars, raids and battles punctuated by periodic truces and peace
treaties. Nor is it entirely right to picture the warfare as between the
English and the French. In the fourteenth century the English kings
still spoke Norman French as their first language and the people of
Aquitaine in south-west France had long owed allegiance to them. So
the concept of two separate countries was not clear. Moreover, much

Map 1: Main sites featured

of the fighting constituted a sporadic civil war between contending French barons.

In the fifteenth century, however, the English–French character of the dispute became stronger. The first language of the English kings was now English. Joan of Arc touched some nascent national feeling among the French. Feudalism was weakening, chivalry was waning, professional armies were on the rise, and monarchs were consolidating their territories. England and France each forged their nationhood during the Hundred Years War.

Today, assisted by the Channel Tunnel and the spur of competition to the ferries, the British make over six million visits a year to France and many spend their holidays in those western parts that the English kings invaded and intermittently ruled. The battlefields, the castles, the cathedrals and the historical museums attract tourists and school parties.

This book is intended to enhance the interest and pleasure stimulated by such visits. It aims to tell the history reliably – though uncertainties inevitably surround specific dates, sums of money, the estimated size of armies, the accuracy of medieval chroniclers, and the borderline between fact and legend. But it is not a textbook.

Nor is this a guide book. While an introductory map shows all the main sites for which the narrative includes a guide book-style entry, the reader is not expected to drive round them all in one big tour! But a visit to Rouen or Dijon or Bourges can be enriched by knowing, respectively, about Joan of Arc's burning, John the Fearless's skull or Charles VII's capital. Crécy and Agincourt can easily be visited on the drive to or from the Channel Tunnel terminal. And visitors attracted for other reasons (such as the fish restaurants) to the stretch of the Cherbourg Peninsula coast south of Barfleur might like to know that here is the beach where Edward III knighted the Black Prince.

If the book increases the traveller's enjoyment, or encourages further reading of the history it recounts, it will have achieved its purpose.

At the end of the book is a set of notes for each chapter, indicating sources that are the work of others on which I have drawn, and some suggested further reading. Any mistakes are, of course, my own responsibility.

Five books I found particularly valuable and enjoyable. The classic one-volume study *The Hundred Years War* is by the French academic Edouard Perroy, first published in Paris in 1945; the English edition was published by Eyre & Spottiswoode (London, 1962). An excellent modern historian's study is Anne Curry's *The Hundred Years War*, published by Macmillan (Basingstoke, 1993). Two lively and popular studies, both also titled *The Hundred Years War*, are by Desmond Seward (Constable, London, 1978) and Robin Neillands (Guild,

London, 1990). The most comprehensive scholarly study – still emerging – is Jonathan Sumption's impressive *The Hundred Years War*, of which, at present, two volumes have so far been published (Faber, London, 1990 and 1999).

Many of the quotations from chronicles are taken from the Folio Society's *Contemporary Chronicles of the Hundred Years War*, translated and edited by Peter E. Thompson (London, 1966).

Michael Starks, 2002

CHAPTER ONE

Edward, King of France

Proclamation at Ghent

In 1340 an exceptionally tall and handsome young man, with long moustaches and a pointed beard, stood up in the marketplace of the town of Ghent in Flanders and publicly proclaimed himself the king of France. He was in fact the king of England.

In Ghent that day King Edward III unfurled bold new banners resplendent with the golden lilies on a blue ground of the French royal coat of arms, quartered with his own English gold lions on red. Then, addressing the gathered crowd, he asked to be acknowledged as king of both countries. He issued a proclamation, addressed to the French people, promising to reduce their taxation and stop debasing their coinage. He subsequently sent an insulting letter to the actual French king, Philip VI, challenging him either to single combat or to a contest between 100 English and 100 French knights.

Edward III was 27 years old, personable, conforming to the medieval model of a royal leader, and an energetic achiever. He was fluent in both French and English. He had always enjoyed tournaments and jousting and by 1340 was also an experienced and confident soldier. He had used the banquets and trappings of court life to build bonds of friendship and loyalty with the English nobles around him. He enjoyed popular support in England. But, to the French, his claim to be their king was both preposterous and insolent.

France had probably three times the population of England and was more economically developed. The French Valois king, Philip VI, had been firmly established on the throne for 14 years. The idea that

Edward III could invade, conquer and rule the whole of France seemed absurd.

So why did Edward make such a provocative declaration? Did he mean it to be taken at face value? Why did he choose the marketplace in Ghent?

He had both political and personal motives. The politics of England and France had been entangled since the Norman conquest of England in 1066. The English monarchy was part-French, it ruled a substantial portion of western France, and the feudal relationship between the kings of England and the kings of France caused resentment and strife. But family quarrels and childhood traumas and humiliations also played a part.

The French Connection

Edward III (reigned 1327-77) was born in 1312. His mother was the daughter of one king of France and the sister of three others. For eight generations, from William the Conqueror onwards, the English monarchs and their courtiers had spoken French (see Chart opposite).

For eight generations the English monarchy had also ruled territory in France. Originally this had consisted of the duchy of Normandy but, a century later, as a result of inheritance and marriage, King Henry II of England actually ruled far more French territory than the king of France (see Map 2, p. 8). Henry's queen, Eleanor – previously married to the French king but divorced after a scandalous affair she had conducted while on a crusade – had brought him Aquitaine, in south-west France, as her dowry. Indeed Henry II had been a truly Anglo-French ruler: he was born in France, he died there too and he is buried in the abbey of Fontevrault in western France, together with Eleanor of Aquitaine and their son, Richard I, Coeur-de-Lion.

After Henry II's death his continental empire disintegrated in a series of battles, which were brought to an end in 1259 by the Treaty of Paris. The English monarchy surrendered Normandy and Anjou in the north-west but retained Aquitaine. The kings of England became also the dukes of Aquitaine.

Edward III's grandfather, Edward I (reigned 1272–1307), acquired

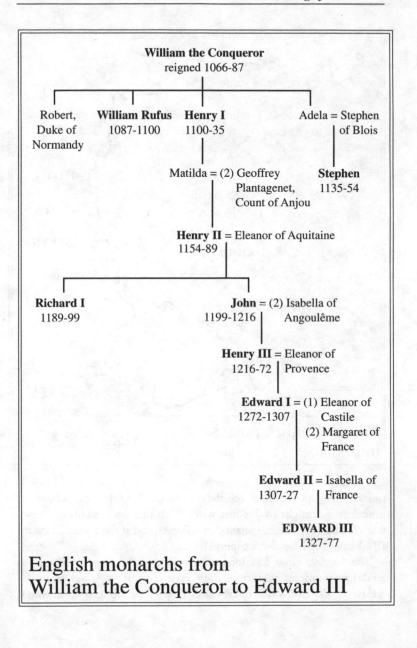

English monarchs from
William the Conqueror to Edward III

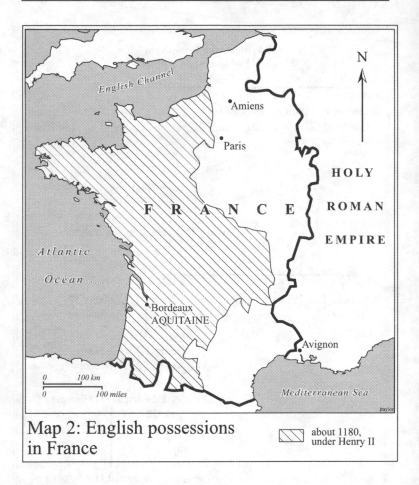

Map 2: English possessions in France

about 1180, under Henry II

the county of Ponthieu on the north coast of France, under an inheritance brought by his first wife. With this small addition, Aquitaine formed the English territory on French soil at the time of Edward III's birth, (see Map 3 on page 11).

The English kings had long acknowledged the kings of France as feudal overlords in respect of their French territory – but from the Treaty of Paris onwards the English kings were obliged to do 'liege homage' to the French kings in respect of Aquitaine. Liege homage was a particularly restrictive form of feudal duty, involving general obedience and an obligation to do military service, if required. The feudal hierarchy also allowed the people of Aquitaine to appeal to France against the judicial decisions of their English rulers. This was a source of continuing friction.

During Edward I's reign, quarrels over jurisdiction in Aquitaine had escalated into war. The French king, Philip IV, had declared the duchy forfeit and occupied it. But Edward I, a formidable warrior, had fought back and regained the territory – still subject to homage. A double marriage then sealed the peace. Edward I, by now aged 60 and a widower, married Philip IV's 17-year-old sister, while Edward I's son, the future Edward II, who was in his mid-teens, was betrothed to Philip IV's daughter, Isabella, then still a child.

A Bisexual Father and an Adulterous Mother

Edward II (reigned 1307–27) was bisexual. His French marriage proved disastrous. According to one chronicler, Edward II was 'too much given to sodomy' and, after the wedding, gave the presents and the best of Isabella's jewels to his favourite, Piers Gaveston. After attending his coronation in London, Isabella's uncles returned to France and reported that Edward was more in love with Gaveston than with his new French wife. Isabella's humiliations continued: later Edward II and Gaveston, fleeing a baronial attack, left her stranded in Tynemouth while they escaped by boat to Scarborough. Isabella was pregnant, however, and in 1312 gave birth to the future Edward III.

That same year Gaveston was captured and executed by his baronial enemies and, for a short period, the relationship between the king and queen improved; further children were later born of the marriage. Relations with the leading English barons, however, remained turbulent – and Edward II's humiliating military defeat by the Scots at Bannockburn in 1314 was a calamitous blow to his standing as a leader. Unpopular outside his own chosen circle, Edward II then found a new favourite, Hugh Despenser the younger, who aroused both the jealousy of the queen and the indignation of the English magnates.

Feudal relations with the French monarchy remained an irritant. Each English king was expected to do homage for Aquitaine and Ponthieu to each French king. After Philip IV's death in 1314, his three sons, Isabella's brothers, came to the French throne in quick succession. The eldest, Louis X, summoned Edward II to do homage and also military service. However, Louis X died in 1316, before Edward II responded. Edward II did do homage to the next brother, Philip V, but only after a delay and with ill grace. In 1322 the third brother, Charles IV, succeeded. He too duly invited Edward II to do homage. Edward was in no hurry.

At that point, in 1323, a 'border incident' blew up into a short war. The village of Saint-Sardos, near Agen, on the eastern frontier of Aquitaine, had been the subject of a legal dispute. When the Paris legislature, the Parlement, declared that it did not lie within Edward II's jurisdiction, King Charles IV of France proposed to build a *bastide* (fortified town) there and a French sergeant accordingly drove a stake into the ground bearing the king of France's arms. The local Anglo-Gascon lord promptly raided Saint-Sardos and hanged the French sergeant. The French retaliated and, although Edward II sent a letter of apology, Charles IV declared Aquitaine forfeit and French troops overran much of the duchy. Feelings of mutual hostility ran high. Hugh Despenser, who, together with his father, in effect governed England in Edward II's name, deprived Queen Isabella of her estates on the pretext of the danger of a French invasion.

Charles IV then hinted that he would not insist on total forfeiture if Edward II ceded him some territory on the east side of the duchy and then did homage for the remainder of Aquitaine. Through a papal intermediary, he also proposed that Queen Isabella, his sister, would be an acceptable ambassador to negotiate the detailed peace terms.

In 1325 Isabella accordingly sailed to France and swiftly reached agreement with her brother. Charles IV would retain most of his conquests and Edward II was expected now to do homage in person in France.

Edward II's authority in England was weak and the Despensers warned him that his baronial enemies might exploit his absence if he left the country. They therefore persuaded Edward II to declare that,

Map 3: English possessions in France

☐ about 1314
▨ lost between 1314 and 1328

for reasons of health, he had to remain in England and instead would confer the title of duke of Aquitaine on his young son, Prince Edward, the future Edward III. Prince Edward would therefore join his mother in France and would perform the homage ceremony. This the young prince did, aged twelve.

Queen Isabella had no intention of returning to England or of allowing her son to do so while the Despensers held power. In Paris she met Roger Mortimer, one of Edward II's many opponents, who had escaped from the Tower of London and fled to France. She and Mortimer became lovers. Together with other discontented English exiles, they started to recruit mercenaries for an invasion of England.

King Charles IV was shocked by this state of affairs and asked his sister to leave France. Isabella and Mortimer merely went north to Hainault, in the Low Countries, and made an ally of the count there. He agreed to finance a small invasion force in return for the betrothal of his daughter Philippa to the young Prince Edward.

So in 1326 the French Queen of England and her lover, together with the young heir to the throne, invaded England. Such was Edward II's unpopularity that any opposition to the invaders swiftly evaporated. Mortimer and Isabella overthrew the Despensers, executed them, and imprisoned the king. In 1327, after Parliament had resolved to depose him, Edward II agreed to abdicate in favour of his young son.

Mortimer and Isabella effectively ruled the country and Edward II was murdered in prison, almost certainly on Mortimer's orders. According to one well-known account, he was buggered with a hot poker.

The Boy King, Edward III

These were the circumstances in which in 1327, at the age of 14, King Edward III came to the English throne. Mortimer and Isabella then formally concluded a humiliating peace with Charles IV. In the young king's name, they accepted a duchy of Aquitaine much reduced in size – indeed little more than a coastal strip along the Atlantic (see Map 3, p. 11). This was a blow not merely to English pride but also to the economy, in that Aquitaine, with its flourishing wine industry, contributed to England's trade. Furthermore Mortimer and Isabella agreed to pay the French king a sizeable war indemnity.

We can only speculate about the way in which Edward III came to terms with such a traumatic adolescence as he matured in later years. Did he feel he had been manipulated by his French mother and her lover into facilitating the deposition and the subsequent murder of his father? Did he resent the concession of territory in Aquitaine, which his mother had made in his name, to her royal French brother? Did he judge that, as king of England, he would need to model himself much more closely on his militarily victorious grandfather than on his weak father? Did some of these feelings play a role in the events which later led him to proclaim himself king of France?

Edward III had only been king of England for a few months when, in 1328, his uncle, King Charles IV of France, died – leaving no direct male heir to the French throne. Charles's elder brothers, Louis X and Philip V, had left only daughters. Charles IV had had a son by his second wife in 1324 but both mother and son had died. His third wife was pregnant at the time of his death so there were a couple of months' suspense before she too gave birth to a daughter.

At this point, after more than 300 years, the Capetian dynasty of French kings came to an end. Recent precedent had decided that daughters could not inherit the French crown. Whether the male offspring of daughters could do so was far less clear. The closest male relatives alive in 1328 were Edward III of England and Philip, Count of Valois (see Chart overleaf). Edward III was the grandson via his mother of France's King Philip IV. Philip of Valois was the grandson, via his father Charles, Count of Valois, of King Philip III and could thus claim descent by an unbroken male line.

The French were later to discount Edward III's claim on the basis of an ancient Frankish law which prohibited succession via the female line. However, the decision made in 1328 was rather more pragmatic. Edward III was a minor, dominated by his mother and her lover whose conduct had shocked the French court. Philip of Valois was 35, had acted as regent in the immediate aftermath of Charles IV's death and had summoned the council which was to decide the issue. Unsurprisingly, the council chose him and he was duly crowned King Philip VI of France.

Two English bishops travelled to France to register Edward III's claim but only after Philip VI had been crowned. When Philip VI required Edward III to do homage to him for Aquitaine, Isabella is reported to have said that Edward 'was the son of a king and would not do homage to the son of a count.' But Mortimer and Isabella had no desire to antagonize France at that juncture and Philip VI could

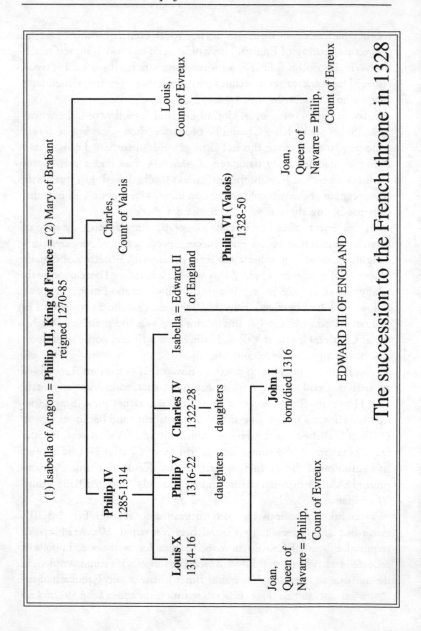

The succession to the French throne in 1328

reasonably have assumed that Edward III's claim was not a serious threat.

To consolidate his presumed victory Philip determined, however, to secure Edward's homage. He sent commissioners to Aquitaine to withhold English revenues from the duchy until Edward III came to France to swear the oath. In no mood to go to war, the English Parliament advised Edward that, in practical terms, his claim to the French throne was unenforceable and advised him to perform the homage ceremony. So in 1329, now aged 16, Edward III went to **Amiens** (see feature overleaf) and, in the presence of a large congregation, knelt in front of the French king in the choir of the cathedral and performed a somewhat ambivalent homage ceremony.

Edward III and his ministers had wanted to do homage not only for the reduced area of Aquitaine that remained his after the peace treaty, but also for the lands which had been conquered by Charles IV in the war of Saint-Sardos. Philip VI's advisers would not agree to this. So Edward III was asked straightforwardly if he agreed to become 'the man of the King of France' for the duchy and the other territories as his ancestors had done. He replied 'Voire', meaning 'yes'. His spokesman then made a speech of protest and handed over a document detailing the English position over the conquered territories. Moreover, the whole ceremony left an element of doubt as to whether Edward had merely sworn simple homage or the more fully binding liege homage.

Edward comes of Age

Edward III was by now married to Philippa of Hainault, had his own household and himself became a father; his eldest son, another Edward (later known as the Black Prince), was born in 1330. As he matured, not surprisingly, Edward III bridled against the subordinate role in which Mortimer and Isabella kept him.

One night in October 1330, when Mortimer and Isabella were staying in Nottingham Castle, Edward III and a small band of followers axed down Isabella's bedroom door and seized Mortimer in a fight. 'Fair son, have pity on gentle Mortimer', Isabella, now pregnant with Mortimer's child, pleaded. Edward spared his mother but banished her

AMIENS

Amiens Cathedral is the largest gothic building in France. It was here that Edward III came to pay homage to the French king, Philip VI, in 1329. He no doubt had very mixed feelings about this, but at least the setting was splendid – and it is no less so now.

It was constructed in the early thirteenth century after a local canon brought home part of the head of John the Baptist from the fourth crusade, and the proud citizens of Amiens resolved to build the largest church in France, 'higher than all the saints, higher than all the kings' to house it. It has a remarkable unity of style and character, which miraculously survived the terrible bombardments the city suffered in both the First World War and the Second World War.

The doorways and galleries of the west front, restored by Viollet-le-Duc in the mid-nineteenth century, are enormous in scale while beautifully intricate in detail. Apostles, prophets, martyrs, angels and the 'Beau Dieu' figure of Christ adorn the central doorway, with the Virgin Mary to the right and the local martyr, Saint Firmin, to the left.

Inside, the nave is dramatically high and light, its spaciousness emphasised by the uncluttered black and white patterned marble floor. On both sides of the ambulatory are elaborate coloured stone carvings of group scenes – with a common theme of execution: the north side tells the story of John the Baptist, the south shows Saint Firmin being beheaded.

The finest feature of the interior, however, is the chancel. This houses 110 flamboyant oak stalls dating from the sixteenth century. Carved on the misericords and on the stall ends and canopies are wonderfully lively scenes from the Bible and from contemporary sixteenth century life. One craftsman carved a figure of himself holding a mallet and added his name, Jehan Turpin.

If you go to Amiens to visit the cathedral, you should stay to enjoy some of the other attractions of this capital city of Picardy. Walking north from the cathedral through an adjacent garden, you come down to the quayside where the River Somme flows through the town and divides into subsidiary canals. This is the Saint-Leu district, characterized by narrow streets, canal bridges and brightly painted houses with wooden lower storeys. A colourful collection of bars, cafés and restaurants lines the quayside, with fine views back towards the cathedral.

A short riverside walk to the east brings you to a fenland area, criss-crossed by tiny canals, consisting entirely of market gardens, the 'Hortillonnages'. There are hundreds of plots, bounded by water, extending over more than 700 acres, all devoted to vegetables, fruit or flowers, and each with its own little garden house. The soil is constantly renewed by silt dredged from the canals. The produce used to be taken to market in small black high-ended punts, rather like gondolas. Today tourists can glide silently through the waterways in battery-powered versions of these boats, ducking their heads below overhanging willow branches and admiring the leeks, artichokes, strawberries and dahlias. While the electric punts are undeniably modern, students of the Hundred Years War can take comfort from the fact that fruit and vegetables have been cultivated on these plots since the Middle Ages.

from any further political decision making. However, he had no intention of sparing her lover. In November 1330 Mortimer was condemned by Parliament and hanged, drawn and quartered at Tyburn. That same month Edward III attained his eighteenth birthday. He was now king of England in practice as well as in name.

Philip VI maintained military pressure on Aquitaine and diplomatic pressure on the young English king. Edward III, having only just seized power in England, at this stage regarded France as a low priority. He instructed his officials in Aquitaine to resist if their territory was actually invaded but otherwise to avoid provocative action: they should 'endure with good humour and fair words, without much argument or resistance, to tide over the wickedness of the times'.

Under peace terms negotiated in March 1331, Edward III declared in writing that he was willing in retrospect to treat the homage ceremony at Amiens as an act of liege homage and Philip VI agreed to pardon Edward for his delay in making the oath. Although no further ceremony was required, it was agreed that the two kings should meet. They did so the following month at Pont-Sainte-Maxence, near Paris, then rode together to Philip VI's hunting lodge. They both said they wanted to settle all their outstanding disagreements about Aquitaine, covering frontiers, jurisdiction and indemnities. Edward III seemed to have no serious intention of challenging Philip VI for the throne of France.

However, Edward mysteriously chose to keep his actions, as far as possible, out of the public domain. Not only did he reclassify his earlier declaration of homage rather than perform any further public ceremony, he also kept his journey to Pont-Sainte-Maxence a secret. He embarked at Dover disguised as a merchant, with only a few companions.

Edward may have judged that English popular opinion would be hostile to his apparent surrender. He may have wanted to keep his people generally in ignorance in order to have more flexibility to change his stance in future.

Edward III was gaining increasingly in confidence as king and, whether in tournaments or in political contests, he was aggressive and he liked to win. Revenues from Aquitaine had always been important to the kings of England, at one point even exceeding royal revenues within England. While he may not yet have had any intention of reviving his claim to the French throne, he probably aspired to reassert England's strength on the continent and, perhaps, to restore English territory in Aquitaine to its previous size. If so, he concealed his intentions from Philip VI and bided his time.

A Scottish Subplot

Edward's military priority at that time was Scotland and he moved his seat of government from London to York in order to tackle it. The background to this lay in yet another humiliating political surrender Mortimer and Isabella had imposed on him during his minority, and which Edward was anxious to overturn.

The Scottish crown had been in dispute since 1288, when the Scots king had ridden his horse off a cliff and killed himself, leaving only one descendant, a granddaughter, whom the Scots had then proposed to marry to King Edward I of England. Unfortunately she too died – so the Scots lords asked Edward I to choose their next king from various rival claimants. Edward I chose John Balliol. However, when Balliol allied himself to France, Edward imprisoned him and decided to rule Scotland himself. Led first by William Wallace and then by Robert the Bruce, the Scots fought to restore their independence and Robert the Bruce trounced Edward II at Bannockburn in 1314.

In 1327 Mortimer and Isabella attempted to subdue the Scots, taking the young King Edward III with them. They failed and Edward was so distressed at the English humiliation that he broke down and wept. Mortimer and Isabella then effectively surrendered in Edward's name, concluding the 1328 Treaty of Northampton which recognized Robert the Bruce as an independent king, returned to the Scots border territory that Edward I had acquired for England, and cancelled all treaties implying any subjection of Scotland to England.

In 1329 Robert the Bruce died and was succeeded by the boy king, David II, aged six. At that point, with Edward III's tacit consent, Edward Balliol, the son of John Balliol, decided to reassert his family's claim to the Scottish throne. In 1332 he defeated David II's supporters in battle, was crowned king of Scotland, and acknowledged Edward III as his liege lord. In 1333 Edward III led an English army north and consolidated Balliol's victory in a battle at Halidon Hill, near Berwick. On his return Edward III was given a triumphant reception as the avenger of Bannockburn and the retriever of England's honour. It was to accomplish this that he had appeased the French king over Aquitaine.

Yet the plot was not fully played out. Philip VI of France offered the boy king David II of Scotland refuge in France. In May 1334 the exiled Scottish court landed in Normandy and was housed in **Château-Gaillard** (see pp. 22–3), a castle on the Seine, south of Rouen, originally built by the English king, Richard I, Coeur-de-Lion.

Philip VI then told Edward III's ambassadors that any final nego-tiated settlement over Aquitaine would have to encompass Scotland and the exiled Scottish king. If Edward III proceeded with the sub-jugation of Scotland, and the imposition of his nominee, Edward Balliol, he would have to face the possibility that Philip VI, as the protector of the Bruce heir David II, might declare Aquitaine once again confiscated.

To Edward III this was a serious provocation. It was galling, as king of England, to have to do homage to the king of France for English territory on the continent; it was humiliating to have to come to terms with a reduction in the size of that territory as a result of French conquests; but that the king of France should then start interfering in Scotland's relationship with England was intolerable.

The Outbreak of War

The Pope attempted to mediate between Edward III and Philip VI. He had hoped to see the two monarchs set off together on a crusade but, given the tensions over Scotland, he cancelled this project. While this was a realistic decision, it did nothing to promote Anglo–French peace. Philip VI had assembled a fleet in the Mediterranean for the crusade and was now free to move it into the English Channel to threaten Edward III. French warships raided Suffolk and the Isle of Wight and a French naval expedition to restore David II to the Scottish throne was mooted.

Philip VI had his own grievance against Edward III – that the English king was harbouring Philip's sworn enemy, Robert of Artois. Robert was in fact Philip's brother-in-law but he had attempted to acquire the county of Artois, which had been inherited by his aunt, by producing various documents that he was discovered to have forged. When his aunt then died, he was accused of poisoning her. He was banished from France and in 1336 fled to England, where Edward III welcomed him. Edward valued a courtier so knowledgeable about France, ignored Philip's request that Robert be extradited, and created Robert Earl of Richmond. So, in May 1337, Philip VI declared Aquitaine confiscated, principally because Edward III had breached his duty as Philip's vassal by sheltering the French king's 'mortal enemy'.

Edward III's response was defiant. He sent an ambassador to Paris to deliver a message to 'Philip of Valois who calls himself King of France'. The letter reasserted Edward III's claim to the French throne and added 'we give you notice that we intend to conquer our inheritance by our own force of arms'. Given the English response, Philip VI's confiscation of Aquitaine in 1337 is conventionally taken as marking the start of the conflict, which posterity was to call 'the Hundred Years War'.

Aquitaine was the main theatre of war over the next three years. French troops captured the north bank of the Gironde and threatened Bordeaux and the surrounding rich vineyard country was devastated. But politically and economically, France's weak point was on her northern frontier, in the Low Countries. In 1328 Philip VI had had to suppress a Flemish burghers' rebellion against his vassal, the count of Flanders and he could not rely on the Low Countries' military allegiance.

Using the family connections of his queen, Philippa of Hainault, Edward III sought to build up as many allies as he could on France's northern front. Superficially, his most spectacular achievement was to persuade – or bribe – the Holy Roman Emperor, Ludwig of Bavaria, to support him. In 1338 Edward journeyed to Koblenz, where Ludwig appointed him 'Deputy of the Empire' for his lands west of the Rhine. This enabled Edward to summon imperial vassals from Brabant, Gelderland and Hainault to serve in the army he was mustering against France.

CHATEAU-GAILLARD

Château-Gaillard is a magnificent ruined castle, built by Richard Coeur-de-Lion, perched on a chalk cliff overlooking a great sweep of the River Seine. It sits above the little town of Les Andelys, to the south-east of Rouen.

If you arrive in Les Andelys by crossing the suspension bridge over the Seine, you see the castle straight ahead and almost on top of you. If you go for a walk along the grassy banks of the Seine, you can look up between the willow trees and see it silhouetted against the sky. But the most dramatic view can be found by following the road signs to Château-Gaillard up the hill from within the town of Les Andelys. This brings you to a vantage point from which you can look down both on the castle and on its commanding view of the Seine Valley.

Château-Gaillard has only a 'bit part' in the story of the Hundred Years War, as the home of the Scottish court in exile. Its fame stems from an earlier Anglo-French war. In 1196, in the days when the kings of England were still dukes of Normandy, Richard I of England had it built to help protect Normandy against the territorial ambitions of the king of France. He referred to it proudly as his 'yearling' since, impressively, it was built in little more than a year.

The design resembled a snail shell in the number of circular layers of protection it offered. At the castle's centre lay a thick-walled tower surrounded by a keep and a moat. Outside the moat lay a courtyard, in which the remains of a well and a chapel can be seen today, and this was surrounded by a fortified wall, complete with watch towers. Outside the wall came a second moat, and, beyond it, a triangular redoubt, protected from the hill behind by a further defensive ditch.

Though apparently impregnable, Château-Gaillard was successfully stormed in 1204, during the reign of Richard's successor John, by the French king, Philip Augustus. After a siege of over six months the French, rather unchivalrously, broke in through the latrines.

Thereafter Château-Gaillard became a French royal castle. Louis X used it to incarcerate his wife, Margaret of Burgundy, for adultery and, when he wanted to marry again, had her murdered here.

In the prelude to the Hundred Years War, Philip VI used it in 1334 to house the exiled boy king of Scotland, David II. Financed by a combination of French and Scottish funds, a small Scottish court resided there for seven years and, in 1339, despatched a Franco-Scottish expedition to attack the English in Scotland.

In 1419, in the military campaign that followed England's famous victory at Agincourt, King Henry V captured Château-Gaillard once more for England. Some 12 years later Joan of Arc's comrade-in-arms, La Hire, recaptured it for the French king, Charles VII.

Beneath the castle, the town of Les Andelys offers the visitor two churches of interest and a walk beside the Seine past the pretty gardens of half-timbered houses fronting onto the river – a pleasant enough place to be exiled.

In practice Edward spent a great deal of money – either as grants to his allies or on the extravagant court he and Queen Philippa held at Antwerp – without any significant military benefit. In 1339 he and his allied forces captured Cambrai and laid waste much of the surrounding countryside but Philip VI's army avoided battle. According to the chronicler Froissart, Philip VI received a letter from King Robert of Sicily, 'who was a great astrologer', warning him against fighting. Edward III wrote to his son, Edward, Prince of Wales: 'We tarried all day in order of Battle until it seemed to our Allies that we had waited long enough and on Monday we heard that the Lord Philippe had withdrawn and so our allies would no longer abide.'

Meanwhile French ships harried the English coast and disrupted English trade. In 1338 a French naval force set both Portsmouth and Southampton on fire. The following year the French fleet raided all along the south coast of England and appeared in the Thames Estuary. A small group of French knights and a band of exiled Scots from Château-Gaillard sailed to Scotland to join a Scots force fighting the English there.

Undefeated on land and victorious at sea, Philip VI ordered preparations to be made for the invasion of England. A 'Grand Army of the Sea' was to be assembled, capable of carrying 60,000 French troops across the Channel.

Edward III grew frustrated. He had already committed the taxes Parliament had voted him, diverted commercial revenue from the wool trade into his war chest, borrowed heavily and pawned his jewels. Now he was forced to pawn the crown he had commissioned for his coronation as 'King of France'. He would shortly have to return to England to seek further funds from Parliament, leaving Queen Philippa and his family in Antwerp as surety to his creditors.

The Cunning Flemings

First, however, Edward did have one diplomatic success; he detached Flanders from its French allegiance. He had started by using the wool trade as an economic weapon. The English had a near monopoly in wool exports and Flemish prosperity rested on importing wool for manufacture. Edward III deprived Flanders of wool and diverted England's exports to Brabant instead.

The Flemish weaving industry collapsed and the Flemish burghers, who had already rebelled once against their count, grew restless again. In 1339, led by a rich merchant called Jacob van Artevelde, they forced the count to flee and ran Flanders as a kind of republic. Edward III offered to resume exports of wool to Flanders in return for a military alliance against France.

The Flemish burghers saw only one obstacle. When their earlier rebellion had been put down by Philip VI in 1328, the Pope had reminded them of their feudal allegiance to the king of France and compelled them to guarantee it with a financial bond. So, according to the chronicler Jean Le Bel, the answer they gave Edward III was this:

> We cannot wage war against the King of France, whoever he may be, for if we take arms against him we are under a solemn oath to pay two million florins to the papal exchequer and to incur sentence of excommunication. But if you are prepared to accept a suggestion we make, you will find a well-advised remedy. This is to adopt the arms of France and quarter them with those of England, assuming the title of King of France, by which we will recognize your right, and obey you as we should the King of France. We shall ask of you exemption from our former bond, which as King of France you will grant to us. In this way we shall be freed from our oath and ready to follow you wherever you may be pleased to order us.

Thus it was that in 1340 Edward III went to Ghent and, in the marketplace there, surrounded by his new banners, proclaimed himself king of both England and France and received the homage of the Flemings. Made in England, Edward III's claim to be king of France would have had little impact. Philip VI had paid scant regard to Edward's reassertion of his claim in 1337. Proclaimed in Flanders, and associated with a change in Flemish allegiance, this time it was much more serious. Philip VI ordered that anyone found with a copy of Edward's proclamation would be charged with treason.

Edward himself returned to England to raise more money, so that he could pay off his debts and secure the release of his wife and children.

Parliament gave him his funds but asked for his pledge that, if he did become king of France, he would never subject the people of England to French rule. In practice, the bigger question was whether the people of France could ever be subjected to English rule.

CHAPTER TWO

The Normandy Invasion

Naval Victory

In the summer of 1340 Edward III was able to return to the Low Countries with enough money to get Queen Philippa and the royal children out of pawn. He set sail from Orwell in Suffolk with a fleet of about 150 ships. Among the passengers were a number of high-born ladies, whose role would be to accompany the queen.

Most of the other passengers were archers, however, for this was a military expedition. Philip VI and his allies controlled the sea and continued to attack and plunder English ports. Moreover, Philip's 'Grand Army of the Sea', with over 200 French, Castilian and Genoese ships, accommodating some 20,000 or more troops, was at anchor off the town of Sluys, in the mouth of the River Zwin, on the North Sea coast near Bruges. Edward III determined to attack them.

The French and allied ships were chained together in three lines, to provide a defensive barrier to an English landing. This meant they had no real freedom to manoeuvre, particularly when the wind was blowing into the estuary. The Genoese captain advised the two French admirals to take the fleet to sea and escape the danger he foresaw: 'The King of England and his fleet are coming down on us. Stand out to sea with your ships, for if you remain here, shut in between these great dykes, the English, who have the wind, the tide and the sun with them, will hem you in and you will be unable to manoeuvre.' His advice was ignored. The admirals preferred to use their fixed lines of armed ships to fight what was in effect an army battle, the Battle of Sluys, on 24 June 1340.

Having spied out the enemy's position the day before, Edward III's fleet sailed straight up to the French ships and hooked them with grappling irons. Edward's archers, massed in the high-decked 'castles' on the English ships, then showered the French troops with arrows. Once this deadly rain had decimated the enemy ranks, the English sent over boarding parties to fight their way across the decks of the French ships, with swords, pikes, and axes. Divers meanwhile bored holes in the wooden hulls below the waterline.

Edward himself was lightly wounded but Sluys was a French rout. About 18,000 Frenchmen were killed, trapped on their ships by the more mobile English. Both the French admirals were killed: one was first wounded and then beheaded, while the other was captured and then hanged in full sight of his French followers.

French corpses clogged the sea, the French wounded were thrown in on top of them and, by the end, the surviving French jumped in as well, and were dragged down by their heavy armour. The fish were said to have drunk so much French blood that, if God had given them the power of speech, they would have spoken French.

King Philip VI was at Amiens and, initially, no one dared tell him the bad news. Eventually, his jester asked his master a riddle: 'Why are the English knights more cowardly than the French? ... Because they did not jump in their armour into the sea, like our brave Frenchmen.' Philip understood: the Grand Army of the Sea was no more.

Naval victory at Sluys only gave Edward III command of the sea for the short term, but, more significantly, it ended any serious French ambitions to invade England, at least for a generation. In this sense it was perhaps the most decisive of all the major English victories of the Hundred Years War.

On land Edward's fortunes were very different: territorial losses in Ponthieu and Aquitaine, the end of the alliance with the Holy Roman Emperor, and setbacks in Scotland. In the autumn of 1340, short of money again, Edward settled temporarily for a truce.

Foothold in Brittany

The following year, however, Edward III found a new excuse to intervene on the continent. Duke John III of Brittany had died without a clear heir – and the succession to his dukedom was contested between his niece, Jeanne, Countess of Blois, and his half-brother, John, Count of Montfort. Brittany became a battlefield for the two rival factions. Jeanne's husband, Charles of Blois, was the nephew of King Philip VI of France. Philip, not surprisingly, supported his nephew's wife. John of Montfort therefore sought, and received, the support of Edward III.

After a particularly nasty siege in Nantes, during which his French opponents catapulted the heads of 30 of his knights over the city walls, John of Montfort was captured. But John's wife kept his claim to the dukedom of Brittany alive and Edward III sent her the support of an English army. Then in October 1342 Edward intervened personally, landing at Brest with another English army to help sustain the Montfort cause.

Edward III's personal presence in Brittany had a wider significance. Here was the self-styled rival king of France actually in France, in command of the city of Brest and acknowledged by the Montforts and their supporters. Edward III now had French allies on French soil. Two other leading French nobles, Olivier de Clisson and Godfrey of Harcourt, deserted the French king and joined him. Philip VI was beginning to lose influential support.

The Montfort cause did not flourish: Montfort died and his wife went mad. But Edward III became the guardian of their young son and the potential enforcer of his claim to the dukedom. The English commander, Sir Thomas Dagworth, continued to harry Charles of Blois. So Brittany still gave Edward III a useful foothold in France.

Normandy Landing

In theory Edward III and Philip VI were bound by a truce which did not expire until 1346, but this had not stopped the fighting in Brittany. In 1345 Henry, Earl of Lancaster (also Earl of Derby and later Duke of Lancaster) landed an English force in Aquitaine and started to reconquer key strongholds there.

With military advances now on two fronts, Edward III plotted a further, and grander, invasion of France for the summer of 1346. He would not rely on allies as he had done in the Low Countries. This time he would fight with his own English troops. His ambition was to assemble an invasion force about twice the size of any previous cross-Channel expedition.

Partly this could be done by enforcing feudal military service. In 1345 Edward had ordered a census of landowners so that he would know who was obliged to serve as an archer, who was obliged to serve as a man-at-arms and who was obliged, by virtue of his income, to furnish a troop of men-at-arms for the defence of the realm. In 1346 he announced that the scope of these obligations went beyond defence and extended to manning his planned expeditionary force.

However, feudal levies could only provide part of Edward's needs. Already armies were beginning to be specially recruited bodies who expected to be paid, according to rank, and specialists like armourers, fletchers (arrow makers) and blacksmiths needed to be employed. Stores needed to be compulsorily purchased, and tradesmen like butchers, bakers and tent makers taken along to support the invasion force.

So Edward III again needed money. In 1344 and 1345 he had secured subsidies from Parliament. He topped these up with loans, not entirely voluntary, from towns and from the Church. Merchants and bankers too lent him money, though Edward had already bankrupted more than one Italian banking house.

In June 1346 Edward based himself at Portchester Castle, at the head of Portsmouth Harbour, and assembled his army around him. He also requisitioned ships, commandeering everything from ten-ton fishing boats to naval 'floating castles'. By early July, Edward was in a position to sail about 1,000 ships carrying about 15,000 troops, plus horses and a variety of medieval artillery pieces including some early cannons.

A logistical exercise on this ambitious scale could not, of course, be kept secret. So Philip VI learned that Edward was assembling a major expeditionary force to attack France but he had no idea where to expect it to land. Nor, at the outset, may Edward himself have decided.

Brittany and Aquitaine – the existing two fronts – were perhaps the obvious choices. Edward would have monitored both Sir Thomas Dagworth's progress in Brittany and Henry of Lancaster's in Aquitaine before committing himself. He also sent a small diversionary force to the Low Countries to mislead Philip VI.

According to the chroniclers, the critical influence came from Godfrey of Harcourt, who had deserted Philip VI during the Brittany conflict, had had his lands in Normandy confiscated, and had then come to England to Edward III's court. He was in Portchester with Edward and is said to have advised him: 'The country of Normandy is one of the most plenteous countries of the world ... if you will land there, there is none that shall resist you: the people of Normandy have not been used to war ... you shall find great towns that have not been walled, whereby your men shall have such gain that they shall be the better twenty years after.'

Edward III took the advice. On 12 July 1346 he landed his invasion force at Saint-Vaast-la-Hougue, just south of Barfleur on the **Cotentin** Peninsula of Normandy (see feature). On the beach there he knighted several young nobles including his eldest son, Edward Prince of Wales, known to history as the Black Prince, then aged 16.

The English fleet, supported by troops, sailed north around Barfleur, and along the coast as far as Cherbourg. The main army marched inland and turned south (see Map 4, p. 34). While Edward may have tried to impose some restraints, his troops began to enjoy the plundering Godfrey of Harcourt had promised.

The English progress through the Cotentin is described by Jean le Bel:

> The Earl of Warwick and Lord Stafford went along the coast, capturing all the vessels large and small that they could lay their hands on ... The archers and foot soldiers followed them along the coast by land, burning, wasting and pillaging everything. Soon they reached the fair port of Barfleur and took it, since the men of the town surrendered to save their lives. But their action did not save the whole town from being sacked, its gold, silver and jewels taken ... All the men of the town were ordered out of their houses on to the ships, for they did not want them to get together again to cause any trouble.
>
> After Barfleur had been captured and sacked, they spread farther along the coast and did as they pleased with the country, for there were no soldiers of King Philippe to oppose their passage. Thus they arrived at a large and

THE COTENTIN

The Cotentin – the Cherbourg Peninsula – has a number of associations with the Hundred Years War, but not many relics, not least because of the destruction wrought by the English invaders. The most obvious connection is with the fishing and yachting port of Saint-Vaast-la-Hougue, where Edward III landed his invasion force and where, on the beach, he knighted his eldest son, the Black Prince.

Set in a big bay, which almost dries out at low tide, Saint-Vaast-la-Hougue lies in the particularly scenic north-east corner of the Cotentin, on a rocky and sandy coast which resembles Brittany and Cornwall more than it does the rest of Normandy. In the middle of the bay stands the island of Tatihou, accessible on foot at low tide and by amphibious vehicle otherwise, and dominated by a seventeenth-century military tower. South of the town stretches a long thin isthmus, widening out towards the end to accommodate another seventeenth-century round tower, the fort of La Hougue. Both from the Pointe de Saire to the north and from the high ground of Quettehou Church inland you can find magnificent views combining landscape and seascape. The little Mariners' Chapel in the town is also a good vantage point.

Saint-Vaast-la-Hougue was the scene of another famous event – the English naval victory of La Hougue in 1692, which thwarted James II's attempt, with French support, to regain his throne from William of Orange. The island of Tatihou houses a maritime museum and a bird reserve. Further up the coast lies the delightful fishing port of Barfleur, which has several English connections. William the Conqueror set sail from here in 1066. Its main street is named after Thomas-à-Becket. Edward III's troops sacked it. Here too there are fine views along the granite coast, both from the Pointe de Barfleur and from the neighbouring, and very tall, Gatteville Lighthouse. It is hard to conclude a description of this coast without mentioning the oysters and the seafood restaurants which undoubtedly form one of its main attractions.

The other important Hundred Years War site in the Cotentin is the small town of Saint-Sauveur-le-Vicomte. Its twelfth-century castle, with a commanding view over the River Douves, is almost worth a history book in its own right. At the start of the Hundred Years War it was the property of Godfrey of Harcourt, the local noble who quarrelled with France, went into exile, and then swore allegiance to Edward III – which led to the French confiscating his castle. It was Godfrey of Harcourt, the chroniclers tell us, who encouraged Edward III to invade Normandy. After he realized that Edward's military occupation was not going to be permanent, Godfrey changed sides again, humbly sought Philip VI's pardon and received his castle back. But he deserted the French king again shortly before his death and bequeathed Saint-Sauveur-le-Vicomte to Edward III. In 1361 Edward gave it as a reward to his commander, Sir John Chandos.

As the war progressed, the castle continued to change sides. The French recaptured it after a siege in 1375 but it fell to the English in 1418 and remained in English hands until 1440. Today the castle has been restored for visitors. Its keep and entrance towers are original and it remains evocative of medieval Anglo-French warfare.

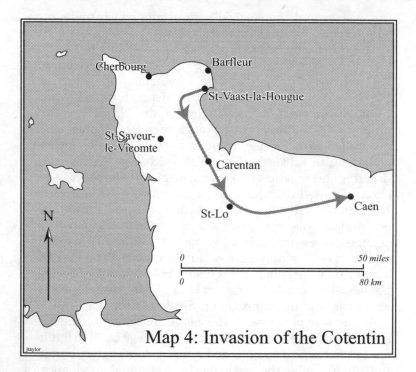

Map 4: Invasion of the Cotentin

rich port known as Cherbourg, which they took and pillaged as they had done at Barfleur.

After recounting similar progress south through Carentan to the foot of the penisnula, Jean le Bel summarizes: 'Why should I recount what followed at great length? The English lords and their armies went along the whole of the coast, burning and wasting everywhere, from the Cotentin to the eastern confines of Normandy, doing as they chose without any kind of opposition. They sent all their booty to England with a large number of prisoners they had taken; much wealth was gained from their ransoms, and with it King Edward was able to pay his soldiers generously...'

Plunder and ransom often formed as important an element in the economics of medieval warfare as taxes and loans.

The first place the English met any serious resistance was at **Caen** (see feature). Bigger than any English town except London, Caen was defended by the Constable of France and Philip VI's Chamberlain with about 1,000 men, including some 300 Genoese crossbowmen. The English lost about 500 men during the attack, many of them killed by crossbow bolts. The turning point came when the Earl of Warwick broke into the town. Even though the French garrison in the castle held out, the English army ran rampage in the rest of Caen. Both the Constable and the Chamberlain were taken prisoner and sent to England to await ransom. Partly to punish the resistance, partly because of the size and wealth of Caen, the English troops spent three days sacking the town. Godfrey of Harcourt persuaded Edward III not to put the whole town to the sword but some 3,000 local citizens were killed in an orgy of burning, plunder and rape.

One of Edward III's greatest trophies from the sacking of Caen was his discovery of Philip VI's earlier order for the invasion of England. Edward had it read out in every parish church in England. In London it was read in Saint Paul's by the Archbishop of Canterbury. Even in the Middle Ages, propaganda was a vital part of warfare.

The 1346 English invasion of Normandy was brutal – hardly in keeping with modern preconceptions of medieval chivalry. Nor did it build any solid support for Edward as 'king of France'. It did, however, effectively subdue the locals for the short term.

The Seine and the Somme

Philip VI gathered his army in Rouen on the north bank of the Seine and then destroyed the bridge, aiming to confine the English south of the river. Edward III's forces left Caen at the end of July and marched to Elbeuf on the south bank of the river (see Map 5, p. 38). Philip VI attempted to treat with him. He offered to restore Ponthieu and the territory the English had lost in Aquitaine, but only on the basis that Edward would continue to do homage to the French king. Edward rejected the offer and set his mind to crossing the Seine.

CAEN

Imagine a park – with grass, trees, benches, an art gallery, a museum, an ancient church and the remains of a palace – all *inside* a castle, then you can picture the chief attraction of modern Caen. The castle stands on a rocky mount, five flags streaming from tall poles on its ramparts, overlooking the rest of the city. The view from the ramparts embraces about a dozen churches, which you see at steeple height.

Caen's history as a town of size and distinction began with William the Conqueror. William built a palace here, the remains of which can still be seen today within the castle. William and his Queen Mathilda also founded two vast abbeys here – the Abbaye aux Hommes, where William himself was buried, and the Abbaye aux Dames, which houses Mathilda's tomb. Eleventh century Caen was one of the foremost towns of France.

In the Hundred Years War Caen was sacked first by Edward III in 1346 and then again by Henry V in 1417. It remained in English hands for more than 30 years and it was Henry V's son, Henry VI, who founded the university of Caen.

Caen has proved a resilient survivor of warfare. It was almost completely destroyed in 1944, after the Normandy landings, when the Germans were still in occupation and the Allies bombarded the city. Fortunately the abbeys survived – and indeed one of them was used as a shelter by the local citizens – but most of Caen had to be rebuilt after the war. The job was well done, in traditional yellow Caen stone.

Nonetheless, for the visitor the medieval sites remain the principal attraction. Within the castle walls, William the Conqueror's palace is essentially in ruins but beside it stands the Exchequer built by his son, Henry I. Like the nearby medieval chapel of Saint-Georges, it is used today for exhibitions, usually on historical themes. Also inside the castle the governor's mansion now houses the Museum of Normandy and the modern art gallery has a respectable permanent collection and an excellent restaurant and café.

The two eleventh-century abbeys still dominate the skyline. The monastery of the Abbaye aux Hommes now houses the Town Hall but the Church of Saint-Etienne remains a magnificent example of Romanesque architecture, unadorned and very handsome. The Abbaye aux Dames has similarly seen its convent turned into a regional council but retains an impressive church of the Trinity with a well-preserved crypt. Nor are these Caen's only medieval churches: Saint-Pierre, Saint-Sauveur and Saint-Jean are all worth visiting.

The modern city too has its appeal – the fountains spurting out by the bridges across the Orne, the pretty harbour crammed with yachts and motor cruisers, the pedestrianized rue du Vaugueux, the elegant *patisseries* and, on Sundays, the throng of the street market round the port.

Caen's other famous attraction is the Mémorial, opened in 1988, part war museum and part peace museum. It addresses the causes, as well as the features, of war and reflects the hope placed by the post-war generation in the United Nations. Having suffered so savagely in the past, Caen is an eloquent advocate of peace.

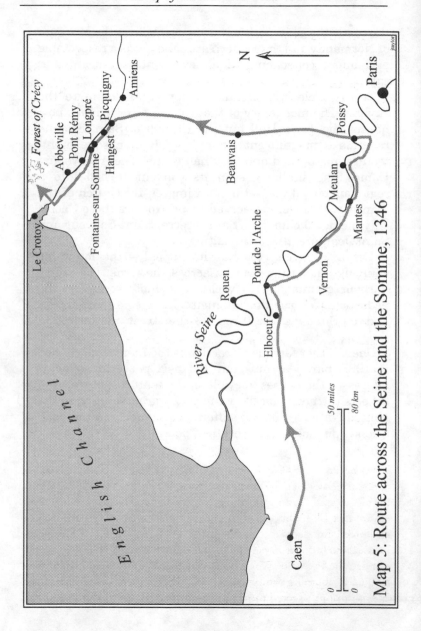

Map 5: Route across the Seine and the Somme, 1346

It was no easy challenge. The next crossing place up the river was at Pont de l'Arche. Here also the French had destroyed the bridge and the main French army moved upstream on the north bank to reinforce the local garrison. The English were in turn forced further inland. Laying waste the south bank of the river as they marched, the English troops reached the next crossing at Vernon. Here too the French had destroyed the bridge. So Edward III moved further upstream to the crossing at Mantes. On arrival he found the bridge here on fire. Again the English marched upstream to Meulan and found the bridge here ruined as well.

Constantly forced inland, Edward III came within 20 miles of Paris – symbolically threatening the French capital and precipitating a degree of panic there. However, he was still unable to cross the Seine and his long line of communication back to the sea was potentially a weakness. A direct assault on Paris had not featured in his planning.

Philip VI consolidated his forces closer to Paris and burned the next bridge the English would reach, at Poissy. Here, however, the bridge piles survived the fire and Edward III ordered his carpenters to rebuild the crossing on this vestigial base. On 15 August he at last led the English army across a temporary timber structure to the north bank of the Seine.

Edward III now had a choice – he could confront Philip VI's sizeable forces in the vicinity of Paris, which Philip challenged him to do, or he could head north towards the English Channel. He chose the latter knowing that, if he needed to retreat, this course would offer him an escape route up the coast towards Flanders.

To achieve this course, however, he would first have to cross the River Somme (see Map 5). This was to prove just as difficult as crossing the Seine. Baulked of his battle near Paris, Philip VI gave chase, moving his bigger army by forced marches to try and get ahead of Edward, to ensure that all the bridges across the Somme were either destroyed or reinforced for defence. At this stage, knowing the need for speed, Edward did become impatient with the English army's plundering. He stopped the Prince of Wales from attacking Beauvais and had 20 men hanged for burning a monastery. But, despite their king's orders, the English troops lingered too long and the French army overtook them.

The French concentrated their defence on Amiens and Abbeville and destroyed most of the other bridges. The English attempted to cross at Picquigny, then at Hangest, Pont-Rémy, Fontaine-sur-Somme and Longpré. Each time the French defences were too strong for them. Edward moved closer and closer to the wide Somme Estuary, still stuck on the south side. Food and supplies were running short. The whole Normandy invasion looked as if it might come to a very humiliating end.

At this point, so the story goes, the English captured a local peasant called Gobin Agache and offered him his freedom and 100 gold pieces if he would show them a ford which was rumoured to exist near the Somme Estuary. Gobin Agache climbed a church tower and pointed out a white path, worn into the chalk, which led into the Somme and which, he assured the English, would turn into the ford of Blanchetaque when the water ebbed.

At low tide, sure enough, a usable ford emerged but, while the English army were waiting, a French force of archers had appeared on the north bank opposite. Meanwhile Philip VI had set out with the main French army along the south bank of the Somme, hoping to find Edward III still trapped and unable to cross.

However, the English vanguard waded across the Somme under a hail of arrows and fought off the French archers on the north bank. After this critical victory, there was still time for Edward III to lead the rest of the English army across the ford. By the time Philip VI arrived along the south bank, the tide had risen again.

The Battle of Crécy

The English troops dried their clothes, had a good rest and went foraging. They rounded up herds of cattle and at Le Crotoy they seized a supply of wine. The next day they marched through the nearby forest and halted on the open ridge of land just beyond the village of **Crécy** (see feature, p. 42–3). With their supplies renewed and now in the formerly English county of Ponthieu, the invaders' morale was higher.

Edward looked at the lie of the land with a view to giving battle. On top of the ridge was a windmill, with a commanding view towards the south-east – the direction from which the French could be expected to arrive. Edward adopted the windmill as his headquarters and stationed his troops near the top of the ridge below him so that the French would have to approach them from below.

In the vanguard was the division commanded by the Prince of Wales, who was supported by Sir John Chandos and Godfrey of Harcourt. A second division was headed by the Earl of Northampton. Edward himself commanded a third force, which was kept back in reserve (see Map 6, p. 46). The strength of the total English army has been estimated at about 12,000 or 13,000.

On the wings of the English army were the archers, equipped with the famous longbow which was to play such a significant role in the outcome of the battle. The longbow had a six-foot span and outclassed the crossbows, on which the French and their allies still relied. While the crossbow could shoot further, the longbow was faster. The English archers could fire ten or more arrows a minute, probably at least three times as many as the Genoese crossbowmen serving the French.

Edward III is believed to have deployed cannon at Crécy too – stone cannonballs were found on the battlefield in the nineteenth century. These early guns probably accomplished more by making a terrifying noise than by landing with any accuracy.

Edward's greatest advantage, though, was that, on Saturday, 26 August 1346, his army was in position, well prepared. According to the chronicler Jean le Bel, Edward 'gave orders that on pain of death no one should leave his place' and then 'gave permission to all to break off in order to eat and drink until the trumpet sounded'.

The French were not well prepared. The strength of the advancing French army has been estimated at 30–40,000 but Philip VI did not manage to bring that many onto the battlefield.

His army was composed of different units under their own commanders – such as the Genoese archers and the battalion led by the blind John of Luxembourg, King of Bohemia – without a strong general in overall charge. The earlier capture of the Constable of France by the English at Caen must have contributed to this weakness. Moreover, for most of the day on 26 August, the French king's forces were spread out in a staggered march from Abbeville towards Crécy.

CRECY

Crécy-en Ponthieu has only one claim to fame – the battle fought just outside the town on 26 August 1346. So, if the local townsfolk want to attract tourists, this is the foundation on which to build.

They face a slight problem: the battle resulted in a humiliating and costly French defeat. But they overcome it with aplomb. The message to visitors is not about the French king's 30,000 strong army losing to a smaller English force. Rather it is about bravery and chivalry, defeat with honour.

The message about bravery and chivalry in defeat is provided by the story of the French king's ally, blind John of Luxembourg, King of Bohemia, who insisted on being led into battle tied to two attendants and was slain. Never mind that he was not French: he is the local hero. In the middle of the town by the Hôtel de Ville, in the place Jean de Luxembourg, stands a tricolour-festooned monument, with a commemoration, on one side, to the King of Bohemia and his companions and, on the other, to all the Frenchmen who died for their country that sad day.

Then, outside the town, a stumpy and somewhat weathered Cross of Bohemia marks the spot where blind King John actually fell and where his body, still tied to those of his companions, was found by the English the day after the battle. In tribute to his bravery, the young Prince of Wales adopted the Bohemian King's ostrich feather crest and motto (*Ich dien* – I serve), still used to this day by succeeding princes of Wales.

The battlefield itself is close by, on a gently rising slope topped by a fluttering tricolour standard and a modern, stylized replica of the medieval windmill from which Edward III directed the battle. Visitors can climb to the upper storey of the windmill and, assisted by a panoramic map, look out over a field of crops or stubble and picture the Earl of Northampton's troops on Edward III's left and the Prince of Wales' force over to his right. You then have to banish the peaceful scene in front of you and imagine the French confusion, the deadly English longbows and French losses of over 10,000 men.

The modern town of Crécy consists mainly of low red-brick and stone houses, with white shutters, grouped round a pair of crossroads and the rather unusual church of Saint Severin, with a fortified 'sentry box' added to its thirteenth century tower. The local information handout says that the sentry box 'may have been built for the Battle of Crécy'. Although one may be sceptical about the ease with which the fourteenth century locals could construct a sentry box on top of their church tower at a day or two's notice, the church has an attractive sixteenth-century porch. Crécy also has a small local museum.

Outside the town, at the mouth of the Somme, the river Edward III had such difficulty in crossing, you will find today the extensive bird sanctuary of Marquenterre. Nearby is the town of Rue, once a medieval seaport, now noted for its flamboyant gothic religious architecture. The other delight for walkers in the region is the extensive oak Forest of Crécy.

Philip VI himself had remained in Abbeville to hear mass and then caught up with his vanguard in the early afternoon. Scouts had established that the English were nearby and, according to Jean le Bel, Philip sent an experienced knight with four others to locate their exact position:

These brave knights gladly undertook their mission, and on their return found some of their own banners had advanced to within a league of the English; they made these halt to await the others, then went back to the king and said they had seen the English less than a league away, drawn up in three divisions. The king therefore held a council to decide on their action, and asked this valiant knight, Le Moine de Bazeilles, to give them his opinion. He replied that he was unwilling to speak in front of the great lords, but that it was his duty to do so.

'My Lord', he said, 'Your army is widely scattered, and it will be late before it can all be assembled. I would advise you to camp for the night, and then after mass in the morning to draw up your battle array and advance on your enemy in the name of God and Saint Denis, for I am certain from what I have seen that they will not flee but will await your coming.'

At this critical point the French medieval code of valour defeated sound military judgment. Jean le Bel's account continues:

The king was pleased with this advice, and would gladly have followed it. But when he gave orders that everyone should retreat with his banner – for the English were arrayed very close to them – none would do so unless those in the van came back first, and those in the van refused to retreat because they thought it shameful to do so; meanwhile those at the rear continued to advance, and thus the valiant knight's advice was wasted through the pride and envy of the lords. They still rode proudly ahead, one in front of the other without any order, and came within sight of the English, who were waiting for them in careful array, and now it was even more shameful to turn back.

Then came a sudden rainstorm, in the late afternoon, during which the English carefully sheltered their bowstrings, while the Genoese crossbowmen pleaded unsuccessfully for a rest. Unable to halt the remainder of his unruly army, Philip VI ordered them to attack. The English archers were ready, waiting.

Some 6,000 Genoese ascended the muddy slope. The rain had stopped but they now had the evening sun in their eyes. They fired their crossbows at the wall of English shields ahead of them. Then the English longbowmen retaliated and mowed them down. Pushed by the French cavalry from behind, the Genoese had come so close as to lose any advantage the crossbow had in range and they could not compete in speed. The Genoese line collapsed and the surviving archers turned to run from the English arrow storm.

The French cavalry, however, continued to advance behind the Genoese archers towards the English lines. Cursing the cowardice of the fleeing Genoese, the French cavalry trampled them down deliberately, trapping them between the French and English armies. In effect, the French knights also trapped themselves – for in this chaos the English archers were able to advance down the slope and fire further flurries of arrows into the French cavalry, killing and wounding their horses. French knights were unhorsed and floundered on the ground at the mercy of the hooves of their frenzied and bolting animals. The rout began to turn into a massacre.

With new forces arriving all the time the French continued to attack, making perhaps as many as 15 charges against the English ranks and continuing the assault by moonlight after darkness fell. They attacked from the front with little direction or subtlety. The English slaughtered them with arrows and spears.

Some French knights did penetrate the English defences far enough to encounter the English knights. The young Prince of Wales, who had never been in battle before, fought fiercely. At one point he was knocked off his feet, protected by his standard-bearer while he regained his footing and then fought on. His companions sent a message to Edward III in his windmill asking for help. According to one account Edward despatched 20 knights to his rescue but, according to the more famous story related by the chronicler Froissart, Edward asked if his son was dead or hurt. On being told that he was neither, he refused to send assistance: he wanted the Prince of Wales to 'win his spurs' and enjoy the honour of having done so.

Late in the day the French king's ally, blind John of Luxembourg, King of Bohemia, informed that the battle was being lost, insisted on

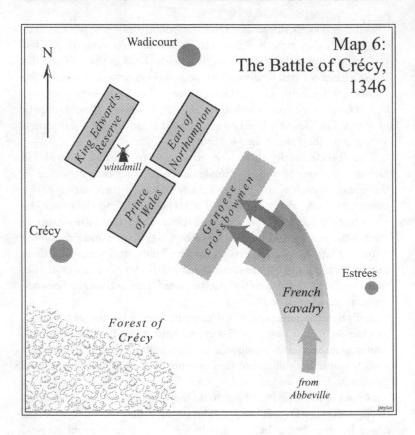

Map 6:
The Battle of Crécy,
1346

N

Wadicourt

King Edward's Reserve

Earl of Northampton

windmill

Prince of Wales

Genoese crossbowmen

Crécy

Estrées

French cavalry

Forest of Crécy

from Abbeville

jtaylor

being led forward in an act of chivalrous valour so that he could at least strike the English once with his sword. His attendants obeyed and led him into the thick of the fighting where he struck several blows before being dragged from his horse and killed. The Prince of Wales found the dead king tied to his dead attendants the next day.

The next day too the English learned the scale of their victory. In the carnage of Crécy some 10,000 Frenchmen had been killed. As well as the King of Bohemia, the casualties included Philip VI's younger brother and about 1,500 lords and knights. Philip VI himself, having been wounded in the neck by an arrow, had been persuaded to flee the night before.

English losses were only a few hundred.

For Edward III, Crécy was an astonishing and spectacular military triumph.

The Siege of Calais

The victory did not, however, establish Edward's rule in France – even over the towns his English troops had sacked or the countryside they had laid waste – and he certainly did not have the military strength to attack the French capital. The French were cowed but not conquered. Godfrey of Harcourt realized that, in swearing allegiance to Edward and bringing him to Normandy, he had not restored his own position, power and possessions on any durable basis – and he was later to switch his allegiance back to Philip.

Edward decided that his next step would be to attack the small port of **Calais** (see feature). In order to obtain supplies and troop reinforcements, he needed to control a French harbour. Calais's attraction was that it was only a short sea journey from England, while also adjacent to Flanders. He hoped its conquest would be swift and easy.

It proved quite the opposite. Calais had stout walls, it was surrounded by marshland and its defence was organized by a formidable Burgundian knight, Jean de Vienne. Unable to capture it by direct assault, the English settled down to a siege.

Again Edward demonstrated a mastery of logistics. Not only did he have to starve the Calais citizens of supplies, he had to guarantee his own. Outside Calais, along the causeway that crossed the marshes, he constructed an English military shanty town with supply lines from both England and Flanders. It was christened Villeneuve-la-Hardie. Initially it accommodated about 12,000 English troops, making it bigger than most English and French towns, and by the end of the siege its population had more than doubled.

Jean le Bel gives a vivid description:

CALAIS

Calais was occupied by the English from Edward III's forced entry in 1347 until its loss by Mary Tudor in 1558. Despite the intervening centuries of French history, it still seems to be occupied by the English today. Most of its central strip – along the boulevard Jacquard, the rue Royale and the rue de la Mer – is devoted to the eating, drinking and shopping needs of English day-trippers.

It is not a pretty town. Heavily damaged in World War II, it has suffered from an early and not entirely tasteful rebuild, with blocks of square houses linked by occasional square arches. The Town Hall, however, is magnificently ornate and fanciful, a continental St Pancras. Designed in the late nineteenth century and built in the early twentieth, its style is described as Flemish Renaissance with touches of English Tudor. The bell tower, equipped with electronic chimes, can be seen and heard in all directions.

In front of the Town Hall stands the famous Rodin sculpture of the six burghers who surrendered to Edward III. It was unveiled in Rodin's presence in 1895, having taken him several years of study and research. Not far away is the thirteenth century Watch Tower from which the French governor of Calais, Jean de Vienne, announced Edward III's conditions for the surrender of the city in 1347. Having been dissuaded from killing or ransoming the whole of the surviving population, Edward commanded that six of the leading burghers appear before him, barefoot, clad only in their shirts, with halters round their necks, to surrender the keys of the town.

Rodin's sculpture captures the inner pride and strength of these six previously rich and important townsmen who, for the sake of their fellow citizens, volunteered to obey the English king's humiliating order and were saved only after Queen Philippa's intervention. Their names were Eustache de Saint-Pierre, Jean D'Aire, Jacques and Pierre de Wissart, Jean de Fiennes and André d'Ardres.

Down towards the harbour is the church of Notre-Dame, dating originally from the thirteenth century but built in stages during the English occupation, hence its mix of gothic and Tudor architecture, compounded by the seventeenth-century fortified cistern that abuts its northern side. Notre-Dame has a more modern claim to fame as the church in which a young captain, Charles de Gaulle, married his bride in 1921.

Calais remains first and foremost a port, with a bustling harbour of which there is a fine view from the lighthouse. The Column by the harbour marks the landing of Louis XVIII, the Bourbon exile who returned to France in 1814, when he thought it was safe after the French Revolution and the defeat of Napoleon.

Calais's other well-known industry is lace, introduced by the English in the early nineteenth century. So the town's Art Museum combines paintings, sculpture and lace.

If you are landing or leaving or stopping to shop, it is certainly worth looking around. Its history is deeply intertwined with our own.

He ... had a lodging built of wood and thatched with straw in which to pass the winter; around the camp he had deep trenches dug so that his army could not be attacked or molested. Each of the lords constructed a lodging for himself as best he could, of wood, saplings and straw, so that in a short time they erected a large and well-defended town. There was merchandise to be bought whenever they wished – butchers' shops, a market for cloth and all commodities as good as at Arras or Amiens, for they had the Flemings on their side and it was from them that the goods came; much, too, was sent from England, for the sea is narrow at that part.

Queen Philippa came to join her husband in his temporary English court on French soil. In November 1346 Edward III made one serious assault on Calais, bringing over a fleet of fishing boats from England equipped with long ladders for scaling the walls. With the success of Crécy behind him, he found it much easier to obtain fresh finance and additional troops than in the past. However, all direct attacks on the town failed, and the English had to rely instead on tightening their blockade and bringing the Calais defenders to the point of starvation.

At that stage the English did not have the town completely encircled, and some French ships from nearby coastal towns were able to slip through the English blockade and land relief supplies. But the effect was only to prolong the siege. Calais could only avoid surrender if Philip VI brought a French army to its rescue.

During the long months of the siege much was happening elsewhere. In Flanders skirmishing continued. In Brittany sporadic fighting culminated in a decisive battle at La Roche-Derrien in June 1347, when Sir Thomas Dagworth defeated and captured Charles of Blois. Back at home the Scots took advantage of Edward III's absence to invade Northumberland but were soundly beaten, in October 1346, at Neville's Cross near Durham. The young Scots king, David II, was captured and locked up in the Tower of London.

In Aquitaine the English force led by Henry of Lancaster had had a run of success in 1345. This had been halted temporarily when a large French army, commanded by Philip VI's son, John, Duke of Normandy, besieged the English at the town of Aiguillon for several months. But in August 1346 Philip had ordered his son north to reinforce his own position. That autumn, while Edward III was camped outside Calais, Henry of Lancaster repossessed much of Aquitaine and embarked on a long march of conquest and destruction as far north as Poitiers. However, he could not practicably occupy this newly conquered territory and, in November, led his army back to Bordeaux, the seat of English administration in Aquitaine.

Henry of Lancaster himself returned to England towards the end of 1346 and then, in May 1347, crossed the Channel again to help Edward III besiege Calais. By the summer of 1347 Edward III had more than 30,000 soldiers and 15,000 seamen trying to defeat a French population of about 5,000.

The English army now fully surrounded the town and French supplies could no longer slip through. The people of Calais were eating cats and dogs. Jean de Vienne wrote in desperation to Philip VI: 'We can now find no more food in the town unless we eat men's flesh … Unless some other solution can be found, this is the last letter that you will receive from me, for the town will be lost and all of us that are within it.'

Jean de Vienne found it no easier to send out a letter than to bring in supplies. His messenger was intercepted by the English. Just before his capture the messenger tied the letter to an axe and threw it into the sea but the English picked it up at low tide. Edward III sent it on, with his compliments, to the French king.

Without food and increasingly short of water, the Calais defenders expelled about 500 'useless mouths' – women, children, the old and the sick – hoping the English would allow them to pass through their lines. Edward III refused and drove them back towards the town walls so that they could die within sight of the defenders.

In July 1347 Philip VI at last made a move to relieve Calais. He marched his army onto the cliff top at Sangatte, along the coast to the south of Calais, where he could look down upon the English forces and the French garrison. It was a daunting sight. Humbled by his defeat at Crécy, and outnumbered this time by the vast number of troops Edward III had assembled, Philip made no attempt to attack. He attempted to negotiate a peaceful settlement but offered no better terms than previously. When this ploy failed, he sent envoys to propose that the English and the French jointly choose a battlefield elsewhere. Jean le Bel reports Edward III as responding: 'Tell him ... from me that I have been here for nearly a year, openly and to his knowledge, and that he could have come sooner had he wanted to. But he has allowed me to stay here so long that I have spent much of my own treasure and I believe I have so conducted matters that I shall soon be lord of the fair town of Calais. I am therefore not very ready to do just what he wants, nor to risk losing what I have so nearly won.'

Philip VI then turned tail and led his army away. The French garrison in Calais, who had joyously greeted the sight of their king's army on the cliffs a week earlier, knew they had now to surrender. Jean de Vienne sought guarantees of safety for the soldiers and citizens of the town. Edward III – angry at the length of the resistance, the loss of English lives, and the cost of the siege – replied that he would kill or ransom whom he pleased. His own captains, however, pointed out that Jean de Vienne had only done what Edward would have expected them to do were the situation reversed. This argument, records Jean le Bel, softened Edward's heart: 'My lords and friends, I do not wish to stand alone against you in this. Go back and tell them that for love of you all I will readily receive them as prisoners, except that I will have six of their chief citizens who must come to me in white shirts, a halter round their necks, bringing with them the keys of the city, and with them I shall do as I will.'

So Calais surrendered, Jean de Vienne was held for ransom, and six burghers volunteered to obey Edward III's whim. Edward took the keys of the city from them and ordered that their heads be cut off. He spurned all pleas for mercy, including those of his own commanders, but, relates Jean le Bel:

> Then the noble Queen of England, who was near the time of her delivery, approached the king in great humility and fell on her knees before him, weeping so pitifully that the sight was hard to bear. 'Noble lord', she said, 'since I have crossed the sea in such peril, as you know, I have asked no favour of you, but now I beseech you on my knees for the love of Our Lady's son to have mercy on these men.' The king said nothing for a time, looking at his wife as she wept bitterly on her knees before him; then his heart began to soften a little and he spoke. 'My lady, I wish you had not been here, but you have made your request so tenderly that I have not the

heart to refuse you. And though I do so unwillingly, nevertheless take these men, I give them to you' – and he took the six citizens by their collars and handed them to the queen, and spared the lives of all the people of Calais for her sake, while the noble lady had the six citizens clothed and gave them succour.'

Exhausted by the long siege the English and French agreed a truce in September 1347. Edward III returned to England in triumph, the most famous military victor of his day.

Although their lives were spared, the people of Calais were all evicted and their property and goods confiscated. The town was repopulated as an English colony and designated as a centre for the wool trade. It became part of the diocese of Canterbury.

After the surrender of Calais, and with its French citizens now homeless refugees wandering over northern France, King Philip VI's reputation fell to its nadir. In 1347, in order to raise fresh revenue, he summoned the political representatives of the Estates (nobles, clergy and commons, constituting a body in some respects akin to the English Parliament). Their spokesman told him: 'You know how, and by what bad counsel you have conducted these wars and by such counsel lost all and gained nothing. As to the losses of Crécy and Calais, you went to these places honoured and in great company, and were sent back scurvily, and you have granted truces while the enemy is even now within the realm. By such counsels have you, and us all, been dishonoured.'

Nonetheless, ten years after Edward III had announced his intention to conquer his 'inheritance', and despite the dramatic English military victory in Normandy, it was Philip VI, not Edward, who was King of France.

CHAPTER THREE

The Black Prince's Prisoner

The Black Prince comes of Age

The Black Prince was reared to fight the French. His father's claim to the French throne moulded his life from boyhood onwards. He was to become a legend, though only in Tudor times did he come to be known as the Black Prince – from the colour of his armour and his horse. In Shakespeare's *Henry V*, the French king remembers 'that black name, Edward, Black Prince of Wales'.

As a child, the Black Prince had been left nominally in charge of England while his father went to war. Edward III used to write to his son from the battlefields of Flanders and northern France. After the great English naval victory at Sluys, the Black Prince was the first to be told the news in a letter from the king, which he then made public.

As we have seen, at the age of 16 the Black Prince accompanied his father on the invasion of Normandy, was knighted on the beach at Saint-Vaast-la-Hougue, distinguished himself at Crécy, adopted the blind King of Bohemia's crest and motto, and took part in the siege of Calais. So by 17 he was an experienced soldier.

In 1348 the Black Prince became one of the founding members of Edward III's Order of the Garter, together with Henry of Lancaster, and a number of other lords and knights who had fought the French, notably Sir John Chandos and the Gascon Jean de Grailly, Captal (Lord) of Buch. Membership of the order remained a reward for military valour throughout the Hundred Years War.

In 1349 the Black Prince accompanied Edward III back to Calais to help foil a French plot to retake the town. Then in 1350 he and his father fought another naval battle, off Winchelsea, against the Castilian allies of the French. This was a large-scale affair, with some 40 or 50 ships on each side. Despite having their own ship sunk, Edward III and the Black Prince won another English naval victory, capturing most of the Castilian fleet, in what became known as the Battle of Les-Espagnols-sur-Mer.

Now adult and in his prime, the Black Prince was impatient to resume full-scale war. But, though sporadic fighting continued, England and France were still bound by a truce. Before it ended both countries were devastated by a calamity that overshadowed any thought of renewing serious warfare.

The Black Death

In 1347 a blend of bubonic and pneumonic plague reached the Mediterranean indirectly from China, spread by rats on ships. The symptoms included black swellings in the armpits and groin, black patches on the skin and a high fever. Death normally followed within one to five days. The plague was later to be known as the Black Death.

In the winter of 1347–48 it spread northwards and westwards from France's Mediterranean ports. The following summer it claimed the life of the Black Prince's sister Joan, who was in Bordeaux en route to her wedding in Spain. In the course of 1348 and 1349 it penetrated the whole of France.

It is possible that a third of the French population died. In Paris the death toll was more than 50,000. Many saw it as a curse from God. King Philip VI issued a proclamation against blasphemy, with loss of a lip or the tongue as the penalty. But the plague did not abate.

In July 1348 the infection crossed the sea to Melcombe in Dorset. From there during 1348 and 1349 it spread throughout England, here too killing perhaps a third of the population. In the countryside peasants abandoned their work on the land. In the cities bodies piled up in the streets and were carried by cart to be dumped in open pits or into the rivers.

People were too frightened to care for their own families and relatives. Doctors had little idea what to do and often lost their lives tending the sick. The medical faculty of the University of Paris attributed the contagion to the conjunction of Saturn, Jupiter and Mars. In some cities Jews were blamed and massacred. Elsewhere religious Flagellants scourged themselves in public and prayed for divine mercy. Many thought the end of the world was imminent.

In 1350 the Black Death eased in France and England – and spread further north in Europe. But the impact reverberated long after the main epidemic had passed, through economic disruption, inflation, starvation and population decline, and, periodically, the plague returned. And, as civil order deteriorated, brigands roamed the countryside. Neither Edward III nor Philip VI could muster the military strength for an invasion, so they extended their truce. Then, in August 1350, King Philip VI died.

John the Good and Charles the Bad

Philip was succeeded by his son, John II, known as John the Good. It is difficult to fathom how John the Good acquired his nickname. He was neither a wise monarch nor an effective soldier. While he had had some experience of warfare in Aquitaine in the 1340s and was courageous, he had a stronger grasp of the romantic ideal of chivalry than of military strategy. Other adjectives which have been applied to him include stupid, insecure, impulsive, petulant, and obstinate. He surrounded himself with various advisers and companions of whom the most prominent was his new Constable, Charles of Spain, an able but arrogant commander, whom John the Good rewarded generously with lands.

Charles of Spain renewed the military pressure in Aquitaine, but without much success. The civil war in Brittany continued between the de Montfort supporters, backed by the English, and the French adherents of the imprisoned Charles of Blois – occasioning in 1351 the famous 'Combat of the Thirty'. The English garrison at Ploërmel, besieged by the French, suggested resolving the issue by mounting a refereed combat between 30 knights from each side on the open plain outside the town. Cheered on by spectators, the participants fought on foot with swords, maces and battle-axes for virtually a full day. All the

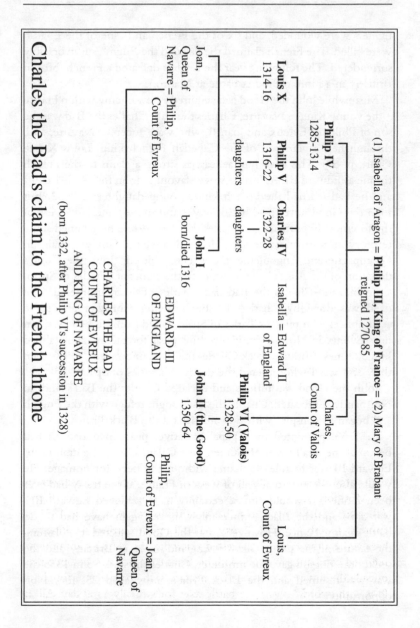

Charles the Bad's claim to the French throne

(1) Isabella of Aragon = **Philip III, King of France** = (2) Mary of Brabant
reigned 1270-85

Philip IV
1285-1314

Charles,
Count of Valois

Joan,
Queen of
Navarre = Philip,
Count of Evreux

Louis X
1314-16

Philip V
1316-22

Charles IV
1322-28

Isabella = Edward II
of England

John I
born/died 1316

daughters

daughters

EDWARD III
OF ENGLAND

Philip VI (Valois)
1328-50

Louis,
Count of Evreux

CHARLES THE BAD,
COUNT OF EVREUX
AND KING OF NAVARRE
(born 1332, after Philip VI's succession in 1328)

John II (the Good)
1350-64

Philip,
Count of Evreux = Joan,
Queen of
Navarre

fighters were wounded, and six of the French and nine of the English were killed. The French claimed the day and the English survivors duly surrendered. The following year the English defeated a French force in Brittany in a more orthodox battle at Mauron.

Meanwhile John the Good had acquired a new enemy within France – the young King of Navarre, Charles the Bad. Charles the Bad was the son of Philip of Evreux and Joan II, who was Queen of Navarre, and, through her, a grandson of the Capetian French king, Louis X (see Chart, p. 57). This gave him at least as strong a claim to the French throne as Edward III. At first he was in favour at John the Good's court and he had married the French king's young daughter in 1352. But John the Good never paid her dowry – and money and land were of the foremost importance to Charles the Bad. While he retained some territory in Normandy, he felt unjustly deprived of family domains in Champagne and Angoulême and resented bitterly John the Good's donation of the Angoulême territory to the arrogant Charles of Spain.

So in 1354 Charles the Bad had Charles of Spain murdered. The deed was done by Charles the Bad's younger brother and some accomplices who pulled Charles of Spain naked from his bed at an inn near Evreux in Normandy, ignored his pleas for mercy, and stabbed him 80 times. Within a week Charles the Bad announced: 'Know then that . . . it was I who ordered the death of Charles of Spain.'

John the Good was furious and declared Charles the Bad's lands in Normandy confiscated. Charles the Bad sought refuge with the English and began to conspire with Edward III and the Black Prince.

In 1353, prompted by a papal initiative, peace negotiations had begun at the small town of Guines, near Calais. Under the draft terms Edward III was to rule Aquitaine without the need for homage. He would also obtain virtually all of western France. If the treaty had ever been ratified, it would almost certainly have achieved Edward III's war aims and the Black Prince might never again have had to do battle against France. However, John the Good rejected it – blaming the failure of the peace talks on England's role in Brittany and the shelter the English gave the murderer, Charles the Bad. So in 1355 the war was resumed and the Black Prince, now aged 25, found his opportunity.

The Black Prince's Coast-to-Coast Raid

Edward III's original plan was for a three-pronged invasion. He himself would go to Picardy; Henry of Lancaster (now a duke) would campaign in Normandy in alliance with Charles the Bad; while the Black Prince would land in Aquitaine. In the event Edward III returned from Picardy within a month to deal with a new threat from Scotland; Lancaster's invasion was delayed by a temporary pact between John the Good and Charles the Bad; so the main war effort was led by the Black Prince, newly appointed the king's Lieutenant in Aquitaine.

The Black Prince sailed from Plymouth in September 1355 with about 3,000 men and landed in **Bordeaux** (see feature). There he was joined by the Captal of Buch and other Gascon allies, making up a force of perhaps 8,000 troops. They decided to raid the territory of the Count of Armagnac, John the Good's lieutenant in the area, in a rapid horseback march (*chevauchée*) designed to terrorize the local inhabitants and to disrupt and damage the economy. Chivalry was strictly for tournaments and set-piece battles; it played no role here.

It was a brutal and ruthless campaign, conducted at speed because winter was coming on and the rivers became more difficult to cross late in the season. The Count of Armagnac avoided battle, and retreated into Toulouse, so the Black Prince's troops simply burned, looted and butchered their way across his lands.

What was impressive militarily, and terrifying for the French, was the distance the Black Prince and his force travelled and the speed with which they took southern France by surprise. They set out from Bordeaux in early October, marching in three parallel columns through the prosperous countryside of the **Gers** (see Map 7, p. 62 and feature, p. 64–5). They wrought destruction, killing the peasantry and collecting booty as they went. As the Black Prince himself described it, 'Harrying and wasting the country, we burned Plaisance and other fine towns and all the lands around.'

Next they marched towards Toulouse, arriving within 20 miles of it before the end of the month. It was apparent that the count of Armagnac intended to stay behind its fortifications, abandoning the surrounding countryside. The Black Prince had neither the time nor

BORDEAUX

While other towns in Aquitaine changed hands with the ebb and flow of Anglo-French warfare, Bordeaux stayed at the heart of English Aquitaine for three centuries. Eleanor of Aquitaine brought it in her dowry in the mid-twelfth century when she married into the English royal family and it was one of the last places to be surrendered when the English lost the Hundred Years War in the mid-fifteenth century.

With England as the main market for its wine exports, Bordeaux prospered during this period and the (mainly absentee) rule of the English kings, who were also dukes of Aquitaine, was, for the most part, popular with the local Gascons. When the Black Prince arrived here with his army in 1355, this was no invasion. He had come to help the Gascon nobles defend and extend their lands. When he returned as Prince of Aquitaine in the 1360s and established a brilliant court here, Bordeaux became his home.

There are few signs left of that today. You have to go down the coast to Bayonne, to the Château Vieux there, to find a building in which the Black Prince actually lived. Most of medieval Bordeaux has disappeared.

The best reminder is probably the Cathedral of Saint-André, founded back in the eleventh century but substantially developed and enlarged under English rule thereafter. Here the Black Prince received homage from the local Gascon lords. Here he used the archbishop's palace as his residence and his second son, Richard of Bordeaux (later Richard II), was christened there.

The cathedral is an impressively large gothic edifice. The fine religious sculpture around the Porte Royale on the north side and the separate free-standing fifteenth-century bell tower, which visitors can climb, are its best-known features. The other main medieval church in Bordeaux, the Basilique Saint-Michel, also has a separate bell tower, which is twice the height of the cathedral's.

Bordeaux also has two splendid fifteenth-century arched gates – the Porte Cailhou, near to the place du Palais, and the ornate and elaborate Porte de la Grosse Cloche. Otherwise much of the old town is eighteenth century. An hour's walk round the narrow streets shaded by their tall buildings can include the monument to the French revolutionary Girondins, the classical Grand Théatre, the church of Notre-Dame and the massive place de la Bourse facing the River Garonne.

The Garonne is, of course, Bordeaux's central feature. Modern port activity is mainly downstream. Sadly, many of the old warehouses along the quays in the centre of the city are now derelict. The modern architecture of the Cité Mondiale, a business and conference centre, has made a start in what is now scheduled as a major redevelopment along the waterfront.

On the quayside adjoining the place de la Bourse, for three days in high summer, Bordeaux periodically mounts a wine festival. Mock medieval tents are stocked with barrels from every famous château in the area. Visitors buy a voucher, which gives them a wine glass and a case for carrying it and the right to wander among the stalls, sampling any ten wines and washing out the glass between each at specially designed fountains. Whatever else has changed over the centuries, the wine trade continues to flourish.

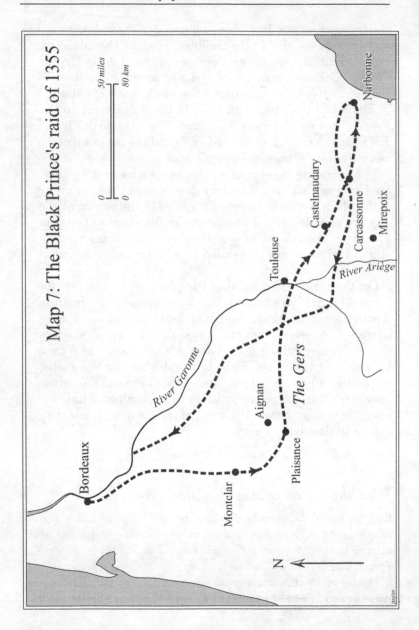

Map 7: The Black Prince's raid of 1355

the equipment for a siege but, instead of returning to Bordeaux – as the French must have thought he might – he pressed on further east, fording the swollen Garonne and Ariège rivers in unexpected and unguarded places. This brought the Anglo-Gascon raiders into Languedoc, a rich area hitherto spared by the Hundred Years War and ill-prepared for it as a consequence. After watching the surrounding villages burn, the town of Castelnaudary sought to ransom itself for 10,000 florins.

At the beginning of November the Black Prince reached **Carcassonne** (see feature, p. 66–7) which had a well-garrisoned castle separate from the town itself. The Black Prince left the castle alone, rejected an offer of 25,000 gold crowns to depart in peace, allowed his troops to sample the local sweet Muscat wine in quantity, and burned the town. Then he led his force yet further east to Narbonne, a port on the Mediterranean. Covering some 250 miles, the raiders had crossed southern France from coast to coast in just over a month.

At Narbonne too the Black Prince sacked the town without capturing the castle and for the first time encountered some local resistance. With rumours of a stronger French force mustering for a battle, he then turned for home but, although there were some skirmishes en route, again the French declined to make any serious attack. The Anglo-Gascon force marched another 250 miles back via a different route, since they could not live off the land they had already laid waste, arriving near Bordeaux, exhausted but rich, in early December.

In terms of establishing English rule in France, the Black Prince's raid was of no significance. But it certainly succeeded in exposing the military weakness of John the Good's government.

John the Good chases the Black Prince

Back in Bordeaux the Black Prince did not rest. He and his commanders used the winter to push out the boundaries of Aquitaine while waiting to learn Edward III's plans for a co-ordinated attack on the French king.

Having reached an accommodation with Charles the Bad the previous summer, John the Good now began to suspect his son-in-law,

THE GERS

The Gers is probably the most attractive part of France that the Black Prince burned. The small *bastide* of Plaisance, which he torched on 19 October 1355, is, to this day, notwithstanding its name, less pleasing than many of the other nearby towns and villages which his army bypassed.

The *bastides* are an extraordinary feature of south-west France. Essentially they were medieval 'new towns', built during an earlier period of relative economic and population expansion (mostly thirteenth and early fourteenth century), and – except for those the Black Prince destroyed – they are remarkably intact today.

Their principal characteristics are a rectangular grid of streets (the antithesis of our image of a medieval town), an arcaded square, a covered market, and a church designed with a simple nave, without aisles or transepts. They were often the product of a contract between a local lord and the inhabitants, providing building plots in return for a commitment to build, offering a measure of civil protection, and carrying a right to bequeath property.

Some 300 of these new towns were developed, mainly by the French but also by the thirteenth-century English residents of Aquitaine. Examples include Mirande, Marciac and, to choose an English one, Montréal. In modern life, Marciac hosts a jazz festival.

A particularly striking *bastide* to visit is Bassoues, which lay on the Black Prince's route as he marched east from Plaisance. It was originally constructed in the 1280s by the archbishops of nearby Auch. The central square has a half-timbered arcade, a well, a village cross and a wood-covered market. The main street actually runs underneath the market hall. After the Black Prince had passed through, the then archbishop decided to fortify Bassoues properly. So the town is now dominated by a 140-foot castle tower, dating from 1368, with a spiral staircase that visitors can climb for the fine view from the top. The tower was obviously comfortable in its day, with latrines on each floor. Today it houses an exhibition about the local villages, explaining the difference between *bastides* and *castelnaux*.

Castelnaux are fortified villages, where a castle wall and towers actually enclose the whole village, providing much more serious defence. Tillac, nearby, is a charming example. Its walls are now destroyed but it has an extremely picturesque arcaded street with half-timbered houses and a fortified tower at each end.

The most complete fortified village in the area is Larressingle. Its thirteenth-century castle walls, moat and three-storey keep protect an unusual Romanesque church and a small cluster of restored houses. The tiny ensemble is almost toylike and, as such, has become rather touristy. A small museum promises to evoke history and an enterprising gift shop offers reproduction Chinese vases, alongside the medieval memorabilia, on the rather implausible grounds that Marco Polo was a thirteenth-century contemporary.

The other attraction in the Gers is the fine castle tower perched above the surrounding countryside at Termes-d'Armagnac. It offers a slide show on medieval history and displays in its castle rooms 'historical' tableaux, including the semi-fictitious seventeenth-century local hero d'Artagnan and his fellow musketeers – and, from the Hundred Years War period, the non-fictitious Thibault de Termes, who fought alongside Joan of Arc.

CARCASSONNE

When the Black Prince and his army first sighted Carcassonne, they must have been amazed. Here suddenly, standing up from the farmland and countryside in which they had encountered so little effective defence, was a full-scale fortified city, with high, pointed towers linked by a double tier of castle walls. It was the biggest fortress they had ever seen. 'Its walls enclose a greater area than London,' they marvelled.

It is no less marvellous today when first glimpsed. It is like a piece of medieval France, which has been magically put down in the incongruous world of the twenty-first century. Clearly it has benefited from extensive nineteenth-century building work masterminded by Viollet-le-Duc, but that was essentially restoration rather than reconstruction.

The fortifications of the *cité* incorporate the château of the local count, the church of Saint-Nazaire, and a small town of shops, houses and, today, restaurants, cafés, museums and souvenir stores. All of this, within the double curtain wall, stands high on a rocky bluff above the River Aude.

In medieval times, as today, the main town of Carcassonne was separate – a large suburb almost – down below on the other side of the river. In 1240, after various battles and rebellions back in the time of the Albigensian heretics in southern France, the French king Saint Louis had the township below the castle razed and constructed a new *bastide* in its place. When danger threatened, the citizens of the *bastide* used to gather together their food and a few possessions and take refuge up in the fortified *cité*.

That was what happened when the Black Prince arrived in 1355. He took one look at the *cité* and, not being equipped for a major siege, decided it was impregnable. Had he known it, the wells in the *cité* were running dry and could not have supported the extra citizens sheltering there for long – but he left the *cité* alone and billeted his troops in the *bastide*. He considered the citizens' offer of 25,000 gold crowns to spare their property, but refused it because they would not renounce their allegiance to the king of France. So, as the English army left, the Black Prince burned the *bastide*, sparing only the religious buildings.

As you would expect, it is the *cité* that attracts visitors today. The first fortifications here go back to Gallo-Roman times. Most of the construction dates from the twelfth and thirteenth centuries. You can do tours of the château, with or without a guide, climb the towers, and walk along the ramparts. While the main entrance for those who arrive by car is across the drawbridge through the Porte Narbonnaise, the view arriving on foot at the Porte d'Aude is even better. The church of Saint-Nazaire is famous for its stained glass and sculptures. In summer various entertainments are staged in an amphitheatre nearby.

The *bastide*, now bordered by the Canal du Midi as well as by the Aude, is worth a briefer visit. From down by the river there are good views of the *cité*, floodlit at night.

Since its medieval castle and towers could almost be perceived as the original for Disneyland, Carcassonne is certainly on France's main tourist circuit, but the crowds are mostly on day trips and the evenings can be pleasantly quiet.

together with his own son the Dauphin, of plotting some form of *coup d'état* against him. How far he was right, how far the Dauphin was aware of the full ambitions of Charles the Bad, and how far any plot was largely imaginary – the product of John the Good's insecurity after the humiliations of 1355 – it is hard to know. In any event, John the Good felt that his position as king was in peril.

Accordingly, in April 1356 he rode to Rouen with an armed force and marched into a banquet which the Dauphin was hosting for Charles the Bad and a number of leading Norman nobles in the castle there. Taking the whole company by surprise and outraging the Dauphin, John the Good grabbed Charles the Bad by the throat, shouting 'Foul traitor, you deserve to die', and arrested him. He then summarily condemned to death three of Charles the Bad's close Norman associates and Charles's squire who had drawn a knife when his master was seized. He had them swiftly executed and put their severed heads and bodies on public display in Rouen. John the Good then took Charles the Bad back to Paris and imprisoned him.

These events assisted Edward III. Charles the Bad's brother, Philip of Navarre, appealed for help to the English – so Edward III despatched Henry, Duke of Lancaster to Normandy to join forces with him. Over the summer they kept John the Good's main army shadowing them in northern France, before Lancaster started to move south-west into Brittany.

Meanwhile Edward III ordered the Black Prince to march north out of Aquitaine into central France, where a second French army was gathering near Bourges. So in July 1356 the Black Prince set off (see Map 8). Leaving a small force to defend Aquitaine, he and his commanders, Sir John Chandos and the Captal of Buch, with an army of about 7,000, proceeded from Bergerac through Perigueux and crossed the River Vienne into the Limousin. As before, they burned and sacked their way across France without meeting much French opposition.

By late August they reached Vierzon and an advance guard scouted as far as the Loire, which they judged difficult to cross. Henry, Duke of Lancaster, marching south through Brittany much further west, sent the Black Prince a message proposing that they join forces in early September near Tours on the River Loire. So the Black Prince turned

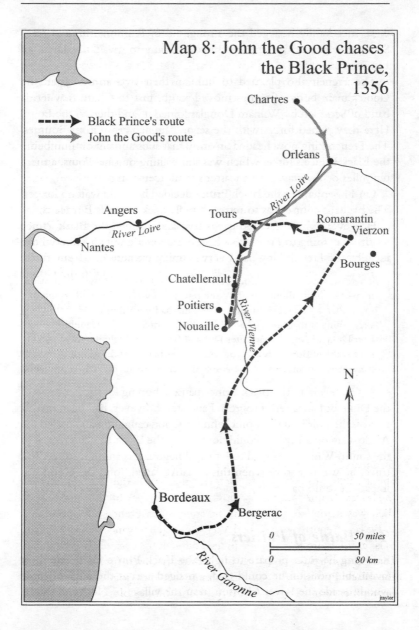

Map 8: John the Good chases
the Black Prince,
1356

Black Prince's route
John the Good's route

Chartres

Orléans

River Loire

Angers

Tours

Romarantin

Vierzon

River Loire

Nantes

Bourges

Chatellerault

Poitiers

River Vienne

Nouaille

N

Bordeaux

Bergerac

0   50 miles

0   80 km

River Garonne

jtaylor

west, successfully besieged the stronghold of Romorantin, and on 7 September arrived on the outskirts of Tours to await the Duke of Lancaster's army.

The French also planned to link up their two armies. John the Good's main body of troops moved south, first to Chartres where a band of Scots led by William Douglas joined it, and then to the Loire. Here they joined forces with the second French army from Bourges. The French king now headed an army that substantially outnumbered the Black Prince's force, which was still waiting outside Tours, a mere ten miles or so away, for Lancaster's reinforcements.

On 11 September the Black Prince decided he could wait no longer. The prudent course was to retreat rapidly back towards Bordeaux.

However, John the Good gave chase and pursued the Black Prince south. According to Froissart, whose estimates are not to be taken too literally, the French king had overwhelming numerical superiority:

> There was such a great army that there must have been twenty thousand men-at-arms, without counting the rest, twenty-six dukes and counts and more than seven score banners. The king had with him his four sons, still very young at that time; Charles, Duke of Normandy (the Dauphin); Louis, later Duke of Anjou; Jean, later Duke of Berry; and Philippe, the youngest, later Duke of Burgundy. So you can well see that since the king and his four sons were there in person, the whole flower of French chivalry was present.

At Chatellerault the Black Prince paused, hoping for further news of the Duke of Lancaster's progress. Lancaster, however, had been unable to cross the Loire. At this point John the Good caught up and passed the Anglo-Gascon army. He could now cut off the Black Prince's retreat to the south. While he agreed to let papal negotiators attempt to secure a truce, he was not sorry when this initiative failed. John the Good was impatient to do battle.

The Battle of Poitiers

Knowing he must prepare to fight, the Black Prince chose the most favourable position he could find, a hedged area at the edge of some woods beside the River Miosson, near the village of Nouaille, south-east of **Poitiers** (see feature). His troops were nervous at the prospect of a battle against such a large French army. The Black Prince, no doubt nervous himself, tried to reassure them: 'Fair lords, we are but few compared with the might of our enemies, but let us not be dismayed, for victory lies not with greater numbers but where God chooses to send it. If it happens that we win the day, we shall be held in the greatest honour throughout the world; if we are slain, I have still my father and my noble brothers, and you have true friends who will avenge us.'

So, on 19 September 1356, the Black Prince commanded his first major battle against the French, drawing on all his earlier experience and on the advice and expertise of Sir John Chandos and the Captal of Buch. The Anglo–Gascon force was deployed in three main divisions (see Map 9, p. 74). The Earl of Warwick commanded the left wing, and the Earl of Salisbury the right wing, positioned side by side to form the front-line. Their archers adopted a 'sawtooth' or 'harrow' formation, many of them concealed by the hedgerows from the French. The Black Prince himself, advised by Sir John Chandos, commanded the centre division behind the other two. Their positions were defensive. The Black Prince did not intend to attack and had not entirely given up hope of somehow eluding the French army.

The French had reconnoitred the Black Prince's defences and formed themselves into four divisions, which were to attack in turn. In the vanguard was a small force of 300 knights, commanded by Marshal Audrehem and Marshal Clermont. They were mounted but, on the advice of the Scot William Douglas, the rest of the French army would attack on foot. The opening cavalry charge would be accompanied by an infantry attack conducted principally by German mercenaries. The Dauphin's division would make the second wave of attack. The Duke of Orléans, John the Good's brother, commanded the third division, leaving the King, John the Good himself, with a fourth division, several thousand strong, for the final assault.

At about ten o'clock in the morning, while the French were still making their dispositions, the two marshals, Audrehem and Clermont, spotting movement behind the English lines (in fact, some of the Earl of Warwick's force trying to steal away towards the river behind the cover

POITIERS

Poitiers was captured in a raid by Henry of Lancaster in 1346 but not held. It was then formally granted to the English under the 1360 Treaty of Brétigny, following the Black Prince's spectacular military victory on the battlefield nearby. But it was recaptured for the French by Bertrand du Guesclin in 1372. Poitiers then flourished under John, Duke of Berry, who was a great patron of the arts, and in the fifteenth century housed the court of the Dauphin, who travelled around central France after the north of France was lost to him.

Poitiers today preserves much of the character of a medieval city. It sits behind ramparts on a bluff above the River Clain and retains a labyrinth of narrow pedestrianized streets around its cathedral, churches, university and law courts. Half-timbered houses, Renaissance mansions and sunny squares add to its appeal.

The law courts (Palais de Justice) are a particular treat to visit. Behind a mock classical facade lies the great hall and the ancient ducal palace. The best view of the medieval edifice, with its squat towers and flamboyant gable, is from the rue des Cordeliers. Visitors can go inside and, mingling with working lawyers, admire the vaulted wooden roof, the flamboyant-style windows and the huge fireplaces of the hall. If you take care not to become entangled with the waiting litigants, you can also go through a side door into the Tour Maubergeon where the Duke of Berry used to reside.

Poitiers is exceptionally rich in church architecture. Notre-Dame-La-Grande has a magnificent facade with biblical figures carved into each of its many arches. Saint-Hilaire-Le-Grand has an almost Byzantine intricate design. The huge thirteenth-century cathedral of Saint-Pierre has a painted nave and lively carvings of animals and rural scenes on its wooden choir stalls. The adjacent fourth-century Baptistry of St-Jean has an octagonal baptismal pool deep enough for full immersion. Nearby are the church and tomb of Sainte Radegonde. You can enjoy a fine view of Poitiers's churches from the hillside across the river, while the promenade du Pré l'Abbesse offers a riverside walk.

The site of the 1356 Battle of Poitiers – the Black Prince's great triumph – lies about seven miles to the south-east, near the Abbey of Nouaille-Maupertuis. The Abbey is in a valley and is surrounded by a moat drawn from the River Miosson. You can pick up a map at the tourist office by the abbey showing a walk along the river through some woods to the battlefield.

This historic site is now bordered by some rather prosperous new housing, but in a gap leading into an open field you can find a sign saying 'Champ de Bataille' and information boards, with maps, explaining the French and Anglo-Gascon army movements. They tell the story of the capture of John the Good and his plucky son, Philip the Bold (le Hardi). No mention is made of the departure from the battlefield, without fighting, of the French king's brother, the Duke of Orléans and his 3,000 men. You do, however, get a good sense of the confusion on the French side caused by the English forces concealed behind hedges at the edge of the wood.

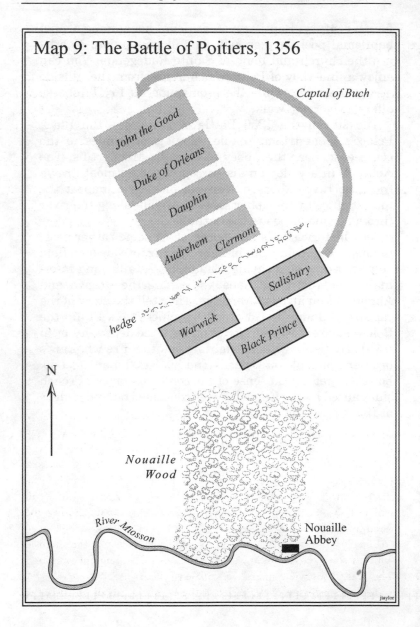

Map 9: The Battle of Poitiers, 1356

provided by their comrades), both charged. Audrehem attacked Warwick's division, Clermont Salisbury's. It proved a rash initiative. English archers, concealed behind the hedgerows, pumped arrows into the unarmoured rumps of the French horses, bringing both marshals' charges to a halt, and then slaughtered the unhorsed knights. Clermont was killed, Audrehem captured and Douglas fled the field, wounded. The German mercenaries following on foot were in turn cut down by English archers emerging from concealment.

Meanwhile, not knowing of the mayhem ahead of them, the Dauphin's division, also on foot, advanced, came up to the hedges and tried to push through. Again the English archers showered them with arrows and, in the heavy hand-to-hand fighting that followed, the Dauphin's division faltered. Probably at the command of John the Good, who did not want his eldest son killed or captured, the Dauphin retreated.

The Duke of Orléans then astonished both the English and his own side by leading his division away from the battlefield. Without having fought a blow, Orléans and his men joined the Dauphin's flight.

John the Good was no coward. Learning what had happened, he led his own division forward on foot, determined to save the day. Froissart compliments him: 'Nor can it be said that King Jean of France was afraid because of anything he heard or saw, but stayed on the field a good knight and a lusty fighter, showing no sign of flight or withdrawal...'

The French king's troops were fresh, the Black Prince's were weary and had suffered significant casualties. An English knight saw the advancing French horde and despaired. The Black Prince turned on him, 'You lie, miserable coward, if you so blaspheme as to say that I, alive, may be conquered.' Urged forward by Sir John Chandos, the Black Prince charged towards the French king: 'Come, John, you will not see me turn back today, for I shall be always among the foremost.'

Equally bravely John the Good swung his battle-axe at the English, with his youngest son Philip, aged 14, beside him calling out warnings. This was the heaviest and fiercest phase of the battle.

Taking advantage of the fact that the French were all on foot, the

Black Prince then sent the Captal of Buch, with a small band of mounted knights, in a half-circle outflanking the French army to emerge on the hill behind them. Suddenly, at a critical point in the hand-to-hand fighting, the Captal of Buch raised the standard of Saint George and charged down, attacking the French army from the rear. The Black Prince then despatched a second mounted force to circle round the other French flank. The shock effect was out of all proportion to the size of the Anglo-Gascon cavalry. French morale crumpled.

John the Good's division started to flee the battlefield. English and Gascon knights chased them and hunted them down. Those that tried to escape into Poitiers found the city gates shut to them. The outcome of the battle was no longer in doubt. John the Good, his son Philip at his side, fought on but he was soon surrounded and a clamour of English and Gascon voices urged him to surrender. No one wished to kill him – they all wanted the glory of capturing the French king, not to mention the potential ransom.

The Royal Prisoners

There was a code of honour in these matters. John the Good was willing to surrender but only to someone of appropriate rank. In Froissart's account he called out: 'To whom shall I surrender? To whom? Where is my cousin, the Prince of Wales? If I might see him, I would speak with him.' As his would-be captors began brawling over him, he called out again: 'Gentlemen, gentlemen, lead me courteously to my cousin the prince, and my son with me. Do not quarrel among yourselves over my capture, for I am a great enough lord to make each one of you rich.'

Meanwhile, Sir John Chandos advised the Black Prince, who was still fighting elsewhere on the battlefield, that he had won the day and should rest and take stock. The Black Prince inquired about the King of France and, on being told that he had certainly not left the battlefield, he sent the Earl of Warwick, accompanied by Sir Reginald Cobham, to look for him. Warwick and Cobham found the vociferous mob surrounding John the Good, ordered them to disperse, knelt before the

French king and offered to escort him to the Black Prince. John the Good accepted with relief.

That evening the Black Prince gave a supper for the King of France and the other captives of rank. The food came from the French provision wagons but, according to Froissart, the Black Prince's behaviour was a model of chivalry:

> Throughout the evening the prince served at the king's table, and at the others, with great humility. Nor, in spite of the king's entreaties, would he consent to sit with him at table, saying that he was not yet worthy to sit at the table of so great a prince and valiant a man as the king had shown himself to be that day. And kneeling in front of the king he said: 'My dear lord, do not, I pray you, be downcast because God has not granted your wishes today. For my father will surely show you all the honour and friendship he can, and will make such a reasonable settlement that you and he will remain good friends for ever'.

The other anecdote passed down from that occasion is that John the Good's young son, Philip, boxed the ears of a servant for serving wine to the Black Prince before serving his royal father – causing the Black Prince to say, 'Well, I see we must call you Philip the Bold.'

Some months later the Black Prince escorted his royal captives back to England. They landed in Plymouth and made a leisurely journey to London where they were greeted by an enormous ceremonial pageant. The mayor and aldermen rode out to meet them; the City guilds provided an escort of 1,000 men and had their members lining the streets in their livery. The houses were bedecked with bows, armour, shields and tapestries. In Cheapside beautiful girls, placed in gilded cages suspended over the route, scattered gold and silver leaves on the Black Prince and his captives as they rode past below. At St Paul's the Bishop of London greeted the procession. Finally, amid much feasting, the King of France was installed in the Duke of Lancaster's Savoy Palace, where he was visited by King Edward III.

The Black Prince had delivered to his father all that Edward III could ever have wished. The English position could scarcely have been stronger. If Edward III was serious about his claim to the French throne, now that he had his rival imprisoned in England, he could invade France again aiming to have himself ceremonially crowned. If, on the other hand, his real interest was in acquiring sovereignty in Aquitaine and extending English territories in France, and his claim to the French throne was merely a means to this end, he could reckon to dictate his own terms for John the Good's ransom and release. In 1357, thanks to his son, Edward III was in a position to achieve the ambition that had precipitated the outbreak of war 20 years earlier.

A Tale of Two Cities

In Paris the Dauphin Charles, aged 18, attempted to rule in his father's stead. The French people were demoralized, miserable and angry. France had suffered humiliating military defeats under Philip VI. Its social and economic fabric had been devastated by the Black Death and heavy taxes to pay for the war were a burden. The coinage had been devalued; marauding soldiers and brigands were rife; now their new king, John the Good, had suffered an even more humbling defeat and allowed himself to be captured. When the Dauphin asked the political representatives of the Estates for further financial support, he precipitated a revolt, led by the cloth merchant Etienne Marcel, Provost of the Merchants of Paris. The Estates were willing to consider further funding only in return for major financial and military reforms. That autumn, to complete the Dauphin's troubles, Charles the Bad escaped from prison, took up the reformist cause, entered Paris, sparked off mob rioting and asserted his own claim to the French throne.

In London John the Good was desperate for a peace settlement. During 1357 he agreed to cede sovereignty of Aquitaine, to surrender much of the recently conquered French territory, and to pay a ransom of 4 million gold crowns. He then urged this 'Treaty of Windsor' on his son, the Dauphin, and the French Estates.

In Paris the Dauphin was losing control. He had been forced to pardon Charles the Bad. A renegade Anglo-Navarrese army had marched from Normandy up the Seine to within a few miles of the French capital. Etienne Marcel was now in open rebellion. In February 1358 he led a mob into the Dauphin's chamber where, in front of the Dauphin, they hacked to death two marshals and hurled their corpses down into a yelling mob in the courtyard below. The Dauphin was ignominiously compelled to wear one of the red and blue bonnets that had become the rebels' badge. Shortly afterwards, he fled Paris.

Then in May, in the French countryside north of the capital, a peasant revolt called the Jacquerie erupted. It had no political objectives: essentially it was a violent reaction against the misery of life in the wake of war and the plague, precipitated by the breakdown in political leadership following the king's capture. The peasants pillaged and burned local manors and butchered the occupants. Froissart's account begins with one such incident and then goes on:

> Next, they went to another castle and did much worse; for, having seized the knight and bound him securely to a post, several of them violated his wife and daughter before his eyes. Then they killed the wife, who was pregnant, and the daughter and all the other children, and finally put the knight to death with great cruelty and burned and razed the castle.... Never did men commit such vile deeds ... I could never bring myself to write down the horrible and shameful things which they did to the ladies. But, among other brutal excesses, they killed a knight, put him on a spit, and turned him at the fire and roasted him before the lady and her children. After about a dozen of them had violated the lady, they tried to force her and the children to eat the knight's flesh before putting them cruelly to death.

The Jacquerie was short lived. Charles the Bad played a leading role in suppressing it. But the popular reaction against such lawless violence led to a wave of support for the Dauphin as the legitimate authority. Etienne Marcel was murdered by his own followers. The Dauphin returned to Paris with order restored.

In London meanwhile Edward III concluded that the French regime was so weak that he could extract even better peace terms. A second treaty was drafted, the 'Treaty of London', and again John the Good was compliant. The ransom remained the same but this time, additionally, the provinces of Normandy, Brittany, Maine, Anjou and Touraine would transfer in full sovereignty to the English king. This meant a partition of France into two roughly equal halves. In effect it would have restored the continental empire of Henry II.

It is unclear whether Edward III expected John the Good to be able to persuade the Dauphin and the French Estates to agree to this. If so, he miscalculated. John the Good had in practice lost most of his power and influence. The French rejected these humiliating terms.

The other possibility is that Edward III, watching first the Paris rebellion and then the Jacquerie, had concluded that France would swiftly capitulate if he invaded with the aim of crowning himself king of France. On this interpretation, he wanted, and needed, the French to reject the treaty to give him his excuse to invade.

The Coronation Campaign

In the autumn of 1359 Edward III led another major invasion of France. Together with the Black Prince, the Duke of Lancaster, Sir John Chandos, and an army of about 10,000 troops including, incidentally, a squire called Geoffrey Chaucer, he crossed to Calais and landed there at the end of October 1359 – unseasonably late in the military year. Their destination was **Reims** (featured in Chapter VI) where the kings of France had traditionally been crowned and anointed with the holy oil of Saint Remy. Edward III had decided to implement his claim to the French throne.

After the disaster of Poitiers the French tactic now was to avoid battle. Fortified towns were defended. As Calais had demonstrated, a stubborn garrison could sustain a long siege. Reims therefore prepared itself well. The Dauphin remained in Paris. However, the countryside was left at the mercy of the English invaders.

As Froissart recounts, the English army had to feed itself:

> You may like to know that on this campaign the great English lords and men of substance took with them tents of various sizes, mills for grinding corn, ovens for baking, forges for shoeing the horses and all other necessities. To carry all this, they had fully eight thousand wagons, each drawn by four good, strong rounseys which they had brought over from England. They also carried on the wagons a number of skiffs and other small boats so skilfully made from leather that they were a sight worth seeing. Each could take three men over the biggest lake or pond to fish whatever part of it they liked. This was a great standby for them at all seasons, including Lent, at least

for the lords and the royal household, but the common soldiers had to manage with what they found.

Edward III's mighty army reached Reims in early December 1359. The defenders shut their gates against it, repelled the English attacks and repulsed English overtures to negotiate. A large army could live off the countryside, especially in the summer and autumn, provided it kept moving. However, an invading army that remained stationary in winter was a much weaker beast. Once they had ravaged the countryside in the vicinity of Reims, Edward's troops grew hungry and cold. Edward knew that without much better supply lines he could not sustain a prolonged siege on the scale of Calais. In January 1360 he was forced to abandon his coronation plan.

In moving south into Burgundy, Edward III found sustenance for his army — at Tonnerre the English apparently drank 3,000 butts of wine — but he did not find a strategic military objective. He circled round to approach Paris from the south but he was no more equipped for a sustained assault on the French capital than on Reims. The English were destroying the French countryside to no avail.

Meanwhile, the French raided England. In March a small French force landed unexpectedly in Winchelsea, set it on fire, killed many of the inhabitants and plundered local villages before departing again by sea. The disproportionate panic this caused throughout southern England alerted Edward to the issue of his protracted absence from his own kingdom.

However, the end of Edward III's unsuccessful coronation campaign was finally precipitated by freak weather conditions in France. On what became known as 'Black Monday', 13 April 1360, the English army, camped near Chartres, was hit by a violent storm. Streaks of lightning and massive hailstones terrified the frustrated troops. Men and horses were killed. Tents were destroyed. Wagons became bogged in the mud. Food and equipment had to be abandoned. With the temperature down to freezing, soldiers trudging on through the hail died from exposure. Albeit from an unexpected quarter, Edward III tasted defeat.

The experience crystallized the question confronting the English: if they could not mount a coronation in Reims, nor defeat the Dauphin in Paris, what was the point of prolonging the invasion? The Duke of Lancaster is said to have advised Edward III that he could easily lose all that had been accomplished over the past 20 years and would do better to secure a peace with honour.

The Treaty of Brétigny

Thus in 1360 the English and the French concluded a peace treaty at Brétigny (a small town near Chartres), which, in substance, was similar to the first of the two treaties negotiated in London between Edward III and the captive John the Good. Aquitaine would be held by England in full sovereignty within a set of greatly enlarged frontiers, including the Limousin and Poitou, reflecting the English conquests during the war. Ponthieu and Calais would also remain under English rule, also in full sovereignty, without homage. French troops would withdraw from all the ceded territory. Seen in the context of the much-reduced territory in France that Edward III had inherited, the Treaty of Brétigny constituted a very remarkable English victory (see Map 10).

John the Good's ransom was reduced to 3 million crowns, payable over six years. He was to be released after payment of the first major instalment, but a number of other French royal hostages would need to become English captives to ensure full payment in due course. In return for John the Good's renunciation of his sovereignty over all the terri-tory that passed into English rule, Edward III would renounce his claim to the throne of France and amend the provocative coat of arms he had paraded at Ghent 20 years previously. The two kings were jointly to ratify the treaty at Calais.

To begin with, events unfolded according to plan. The Dauphin, probably reluctantly, ratified the treaty and so did the Black Prince, who became Prince of Aquitaine. The first ransom payment was made. The two kings met in Calais but here, instead of completing the renunciations, they addressed the difficulties encountered in complet-ing the territorial transfers – problems of removing French troops from the areas that were to be English and withdrawing English troops from the remaining parts of France. The two kings now agreed to complete the renunciations formally either when all the territorial transfers were

Map 10: English possessions in France

in 1360, under the Treaty of Brétigny

achieved or in November 1361, whichever was the sooner. They also agreed that John the Good's sons, Louis of Anjou and John of Berry, together with the Duke of Orléans and the Duke of Bourbon, would act as hostages until the next major instalment of the ransom had been paid.

November 1361 passed without any formal resolution of the sovereignty issue. In 1362 the royal princes negotiated parole for themselves in Calais by promising some further concessions, which were accepted by John the Good but not by the Dauphin or the Estates. Then in 1363 one of the royal hostages, Louis of Anjou, who had married just before he became a hostage and had not seen his young wife since, broke his parole and refused to return. John the Good was angry and ashamed and, in honour, felt obliged to surrender himself back into captivity. So in January 1364 the king of France once more became a prisoner in England, awaiting the full payment of his ransom.

Then, a few months later, in April 1364, John the Good died, still an English captive. The formal renunciations remained incomplete.

Differently implemented, the Treaty of Brétigny might have ended the Anglo-French conflict. The Black Prince's capture of the French king at Poitiers had certainly presented Edward III with an ideal opportunity. As it was, the death of John the Good as a prisoner in England left unresolved the two main questions underlying the Hundred Years War: which king was sovereign in Aquitaine and was the king of England serious in claiming to be the king of France?

CHAPTER FOUR

Resistance and Reconciliation

Charles the Wise and his General

The new king of France, Charles V, was frail and sickly. At the age of 18 he had taken part in the Battle of Poitiers, when his father had been captured, but shortly afterwards he had contracted a mysterious disease, which made him easily exhausted and forced him to retire to bed. He found riding difficult and did not travel much. Nor did he fight in battle again. He was the complete antithesis of the warrior-king Edward III of England and his warrior son, the Black Prince. Yet he was to defeat them.

Charles was clever. He was an intellectual who loved his extensive library – and he became known to history as Charles the Wise essentially because of his erudition. He was wise, not to say cunning, in politics and diplomacy too. During the years of his father's captivity his life was made a misery by Charles the Bad and Etienne Marcel, but, through perseverance and budding political skill, he out-manoeuvred them both. He learned when to bide his time and when to strike. He learned how to use the law to advantage. He learned how to use others to secure ends he could not achieve personally.

Foremost among those who served him was a squat, ugly Breton captain of low birth called Bertrand du Guesclin, whom Charles V recognized as a professional soldier capable of leading the French army. Du Guesclin became a legend and his early life is now surrounded by a certain amount of myth. He was born near **Dinan** (see feature) in Brittany in the early 1320s. He is said to have been an outcast within his family as a result of his ugliness, to have been illiterate, to have run away

DINAN

Dinan, seat of the dukes of Brittany, featured prominently in the Breton civil wars. Its most famous connection with the Hundred Years War, however, is as the home of Bertrand du Guesclin, France's only real military hero of its unhappy fourteenth century. He was born nearby, wed his wife here, and it was here that he asked to be buried.

A lively equestrian statue, which does justice to du Guesclin's somewhat unprepossessing appearance, rises above the pollarded trees of the town's large open square. Here du Guesclin fought his legendary single combat against the English knight, Thomas of Canterbury. The Duke of Lancaster was besieging Dinan at the time but had agreed to a truce, which Thomas of Canterbury had broken by capturing du Guesclin's brother, Olivier, for ransom. A furious du Guesclin challenged and defeated Canterbury here in the place du Champ-Clos. Lancaster ordered Olivier to be freed and compensated, Canterbury was disgraced and du Guesclin accepted a cup of *vin d'honneur* before returning to his own side. His victory had been predicted by the local astrologer, Tiphaine de Raguenel, whom du Guesclin later met and married.

High on a hill above the River Rance, Dinan is a splendid example of a medieval fortified town. The Keep, where the Dukes of Brittany once resided, is joined to several other fortified towers by thick, high ramparts. You can walk most of the way round them by following three promenades. The Keep has now been converted into a museum.

From the thirteenth-century Tour Sainte-Catherine, or from the adjoining Jardin Anglais, you have an eagle's eye view of the small port of Dinan on the riverbank below. Once a thriving commercial centre, it is now a colourful collection of moored yachts, tourist boats, cafés and restaurants. You can walk down to it on the steep cobbled rue de Jerzual, with its half-timbered medieval houses, through the Jerzual Gate into the rue du Petit Fort and on past the fifteenth-century Maison du Gouverneur.

The centre of Dinan too contains several picturesque medieval streets, concentrated around the place des Merciers, L'Apport and the place des Cordeliers. A three-storey, and rather crooked, clock tower adds to the character of the area.

Adjacent are Dinan's two principal churches. The church of Saint-Malo, the local saint, was started in the fifteenth century but only completed in the nineteenth. Opposite (to digress briefly) is the most wonderful bakery – even by French standards – with traditional wood-heated ovens into which the bread is pushed with long-handled shovels.

The older and more distinguished church is the Basili-que Saint-Sauveur. It too has a curious mix of styles. The weathered statues of lions and bulls set into the colon-nades of the west front reflect eastern influences stem-ming from the crusades. The nave has a twelfth-century wall on one side and a fifteenth-century wall on the other. Dotted around the interior are baroque altars. In the north transept, underneath a nineteenth-century painting depicting his death, stands the tomb of Bertrand du Guesclin. King Charles V insisted that du Guesclin's body was buried at Saint-Denis but his heart at least was brought back to Dinan as he wished. It was buried first in a nearby Dominican church but, when this was destroyed in the French Revolution, moved here to Saint-Sauveur. More eloquent than the gold script on the tombstone is the double-headed eagle with a red stripe, which du Guesclin made his emblem.

from home to his uncle's house, to have made his name fighting in tournaments (in one of which he remained mysteriously anonymous to avoid being recognized by his father) and to have financed his first band of soldiers by stealing and selling his mother's jewels. He fought for Charles of Blois in Brittany's civil war. He exhibited characteristic adventurism and cunning in capturing the stronghold of Fougeray by disguising his band of soldiers as peasants carrying bundles of wood and taking the garrison by surprise. He impeded Henry of Lancaster's siege of Rennes in 1356–57. At the time of Charles V's accession in 1364 he was fighting on the Seine against the Navarrese forces of Charles the Bad.

It was then, just after the death of John the Good, that the Captal of Buch led an Anglo-Gascon-Navarrese troop of about 1,500 or 2,000 men out of Normandy towards the Seine with the aim of disrupting or preventing Charles V's coronation at Reims. Du Guesclin blocked their progress with a French force of perhaps 1,200. In the ensuing battle of Cocherel, du Guesclin outwitted and outflanked the Captal and took him prisoner. After his coronation, Charles V thanked du Guesclin warmly, rewarded him with land and title and formed a professional bond between politician and soldier, which was to last the rest of their lives. Charles V was probably resolved from the very outset of his reign to expel the English from the territory they had acquired under the humiliating Treaty of Brétigny, but he set out to strengthen his political and military position first.

His first success followed a military setback in Brittany where rival claimants were still contesting the dukedom. In September 1364, the English general Sir John Chandos, supporting John of Montfort (to whom Edward III had been a guardian), soundly defeated the French candidate, Charles of Blois, and du Guesclin at the battle of Auray. Charles of Blois himself was killed and du Guesclin captured. On Charles of Blois' death, John of Montfort was the obvious, and only practical, bearer of the title of duke of Brittany. Displaying his political cunning, Charles V persuaded Montfort to switch his allegiance from England to France, in return for formal French recognition of his position. He also paid du Guesclin's ransom.

Charles V secured another diplomatic victory later the same year –

the marriage of his young brother, Philip the Bold, Duke of Burgundy, to Margaret of Flanders, the richest heiress in Europe (to whom Edward III had earlier attempted to marry one of his sons). In later years an enlarged dukedom of Burgundy was to prove a threat to the French monarchy but, for Charles V, the more immediate result was to ensure that Flanders would side with France, not England, should the Anglo-French conflict restart.

Pied Piper of the Free Companies

Charles V had a new role in mind for du Guesclin for 1365. He asked him to act as a pied piper to help rid France of the menace of the bands of mercenaries sometimes known as the 'Free Companies', and also termed the *routiers*.

The wars in France triggered by Edward III's claim to the French throne had been fought, to a much greater extent than earlier conflicts, by professional soldiers. Men had enlisted in return for a wage, the opportunity of plunder and the proceeds from the ransom of any distinguished prisoners they managed to capture. Over the 1340s and 1350s for many – Englishmen, Frenchmen, Gascons, Bretons, Navarrese and a few Scots – warfare in France became a way of life. They were not peasants who had left tilling the soil temporarily to fulfil their feudal duty by fighting for a season. They were essentially mercenaries, whose conduct at times bordered on that of robbers and plunderers. The warfare in Aquitaine, characterized by swift sharp raids more than by set-piece battles, was a breeding ground for Gascon adventurism of this kind. One of the most notorious adventurers, Arnaud de Cervole, nicknamed the Archpriest, formed a makeshift army called the Great Company, which he led on a looting expedition into Provence.

With the Treaty of Brétigny and the end of the official war, these mercenaries had no other trade to which to return. Many remained, therefore, roaming at large through France, essentially as robbers and bandits. In the early 1360s, when civil administration was disrupted by the (often locally disputed) transfers of territory under the terms of the peace treaty, there was no strong authority to restrict their lawlessness.

An attempt by the Pope to persuade Arnaud de Cervole to lead his underemployed brigands on a crusade against the Turks collapsed almost at the outset. The Duke of Bourbon was killed when he confronted a mercenary band near Lyons in 1363. The Free Companies were out of control.

So in 1365 Charles V asked Bertrand du Guesclin to round up as large an army as he could from among these wandering mercenaries and lead them across the Pyrenees into Spain on a specific mission. They were to depose the King of Castile, Pedro the Cruel, and replace him on the throne by his bastard half-brother, Henry of Trastamara. Pedro had married Charles V's sister-in-law, Blanche of Bourbon, and subsequently locked her up in prison and had her killed. He was also in conflict with the king of Aragon over some frontier provinces. Charles V saw an opportunity to ally with Aragon and impose his own candidate on the throne of Castile. The expedition could rid France of the worst excesses of the Free Companies. Moreover, with a French ally as king of Castile, the Castilian navy could again be deployed against England, were the Anglo-French war to re-open.

Pedro was so unpopular in Castile that du Guesclin's expedition was swiftly successful. Pedro fled, Henry of Trastamara took his place, du Guesclin was made a Spanish duke and his army of mercenaries was well rewarded.

Pedro and the Black Prince

Since becoming Prince of Aquitaine in the aftermath of the Treaty of Brétigny, the Black Prince had set up court in Bordeaux. In 1361 he had married Joan of Kent and their second son, Richard, was born in Bordeaux. The Black Prince and his princess lived there in grand style, surrounded by a set of English lords and a large retinue, moving between Bordeaux, Angoulême and Poitiers in an extravagant round of banquets and tournaments, financed by the income from local taxes.

It was to the Black Prince that the deposed Pedro the Cruel fled for help. Pedro asked the Black Prince to lead an army through Navarre – where they would have the support of Charles the Bad – into Castile, to confront du Guesclin and overthrow the usurper, Henry of

Trastamara. The Black Prince was sympathetic. He was aware of the dangers of having a French puppet on the Castilian throne. In Aquitaine he too had plenty of unemployed soldiers who would welcome another fight. However, he would only undertake the expedition if Pedro would reimburse the very heavy costs that would be incurred. Pedro pledged to do so, provided the Black Prince won. The Black Prince confidently agreed.

In January 1367 the Black Prince set off for Dax, in the foothills of the Pyrenees, where his expeditionary army was gathering. Here he joined his younger brother, John of Gaunt. John was a child of the Anglo-French war, in that he had been born at Ghent (Gaunt = Ghent) when Edward III left Queen Philippa there in 1340. He had married into Henry of Lancaster's family and, after Henry's death from the plague in 1362, become heir to the title of Duke of Lancaster. He was now ready to follow in his father's and brother's military footsteps. He sailed from England to Cherbourg with his own contingent of troops and marched them south through France to Dax. Sir John Chandos, now Constable of Aquitaine, was also there. Under the Black Prince's command, they assembled perhaps as many as 10,000 troops.

After some earlier skirmishing, the main battle with du Guesclin and Henry of Trastamara took place near the town of Najera in Castile on 3 April 1367. The Black Prince took his opponents by surprise and Chandos and John of Gaunt withstood du Guesclin's counter-attack. It proved another English military triumph. Henry of Trastamara fled the field, with half his army dead, and du Guesclin was captured. Pedro the Cruel was restored to his throne. The Black Prince's reputation as western Europe's most formidable warrior was reinforced.

Yet this whole expedition was the Black Prince's greatest mistake. Pedro the Cruel never paid his debt, reckoned to have been 2,720,000 florins. Henry of Trastamara returned to Castile the following year, tricked Pedro into meeting him, and personally murdered him. Moreover, while in Spain the Black Prince contracted a disease, probably either dysentery or malaria, from which he never recovered. Ill health was to dominate the remaining years of his life.

French Resistance

Pedro's unpaid debt triggered a series of events which re-opened the war. The Black Prince's regime in Bordeaux was never entirely popular with the locals. When their English overlord was far away across the sea, English rule in Aquitaine left the local lords with responsibility and power without any close supervision. But, when the Black Prince arrived to take up residence, he awarded positions of authority under him to Englishmen instead. He was also extravagant in his expenditure and correspondingly heavy handed in his demands for local taxation. In three successive years – 1364, 1365 and 1366 – he had levied an unpopular hearth tax.

When the Black Prince returned from Spain without any reimbursement from Pedro, local loyalties became seriously strained. First, he was unable to reward his followers who, of course, had expected to profit substantially from accompanying him on his Spanish expedition. Second, he was now extremely short of funds himself. The cost of his Spanish expedition had exceeded by several times the revenue he received in a year. He had no reserve. He was essentially bankrupt. His only recourse was to seek a further increase in taxation from his Aquitaine subjects. In 1368 he demanded that the hearth tax become permanent for at least five years in order to pay off his debts.

Two leading nobles, the Count of Armagnac and the Lord of Albret, refused to have this tax levied in their territories. They appealed to King Edward III of England but, more significantly, they inquired whether they could lodge an appeal with King Charles V of France.

Charles V had been quietly preparing for a resumption of the Anglo-French war. He had replenished his own exchequer. He had once again paid du Guesclin's ransom. He had ordered an enquiry into how many archers each French town could provide; made military training mandatory; required his lords to keep their castles in good defensive condition; and commissioned new warships. He knew that, if he agreed to hear the appeal of the two Gascon lords against the Black Prince's taxation, he would be repudiating the agreement at the time of the Treaty of Brétigny that Aquitaine would be held by the King of England in full sovereignty.

Charles V was now ready to do this but keen, first, to ensure that he could claim to be acting legally. So he called in his lawyers. They recollected that the Treaty of Brétigny itself had not fully implemented the agreement whereby the king of England was to renounce his claim to the French throne and the king of France was to renounce sovereignty over Aquitaine. At the subsequent meeting of Edward III and John the Good at Calais, it had been agreed that this process would be completed either when all the territorial transfers had been achieved or in November 1361, whichever was the sooner. In fact the transfers had dragged on well past that date. In practice, Edward III stopped calling himself king of France and no longer quartered the French royal coat of arms with his own, but November 1361 had passed without any formal renunciation of his claim.

Since the renunciations had never been formalized, the French lawyers reasoned, it followed that Charles V could plausibly maintain that, legally, he was still the overlord of Aquitaine. On that basis he could hear the Gascon lords' appeal. However, on this interpretation, he would also have to recognize that Edward III had not formally renounced his claim to the French throne. He must also expect a decision to hear the appeal to precipitate war.

This was what Charles V wanted. He almost certainly colluded with the Gascon lords in formulating the grounds of the appeal. It was addressed to the French king 'in his capacity as the sovereign lord of the Duke and the whole duchy of Aquitaine'.

Charles V's next move was to encourage many more appeals and, over the following months, he received nearly a thousand – from all over Aquitaine. He scheduled a hearing of the issue in his presence in May 1369 and summoned the Black Prince to appear before him in Paris.

Legend has it that the Black Prince replied: 'We will willingly go to Paris on the day we are cited to be there, since the king of France commands it, but it will be with our helmet on our head and 60,000 men in our company.'

If true, there was a strong element of bravado here because the Black Prince was now very seriously ill. But he certainly could not acquiesce. In London Edward III reasserted his claim to be king of France and added the arms of France back into his English coat of arms. Charles V declared the duchy of Aquitaine confiscated.

France overturns the English Conquests

Edward III was now in his late fifties. His wife, Queen Philippa, died in 1369. In the later years of his reign Edward fell increasingly under the influence of his mistress, Alice Perrers. He was too old, physically and mentally, to lead a fresh English invasion of France.

That responsibility now passed to John of Gaunt, Duke of Lancaster. At the end of 1369 John of Gaunt landed at Calais and marched through Picardy into Normandy. The French avoided battle and, with the onset of winter, Gaunt was forced to retreat, having accomplished nothing.

The following year, 1370, a leader of much lower birth, the knight Sir Robert Knowles, led a further French invasion. He marched boldly towards Paris but du Guesclin, now promoted to be Constable of France, forced him to retreat towards Brittany, followed him, and defeated him soundly at Pontvallain, near Le Mans.

Meanwhile, the French admiral, Jean de Vienne, veteran of the 1347 siege of Calais, raided the English coast. The French also reconquered large tracts of territory in Aquitaine in 1369 and 1370 and a French soldier killed Sir John Chandos, the English commander there, in hand-to-hand fighting.

French forces then laid siege to the city of Limoges, where English authority was vested in the bishop, an ally of the Black Prince and godfather to one of his children. The Bishop of Limoges negotiated the surrender of the city. The Black Prince was furious at this almost personal betrayal and, though ill, had himself carried to Limoges in a litter on an expedition of revenge. His troops spent a month mining the fortified walls of the city and, as Froissart relates:

> When they knew it was the right time for it, the miners started a fire in their mine. In the morning, just as the Prince had specified, a great section of the wall collapsed, filling the moat at the place where it fell. For the English, who were armed and ready waiting, it was a welcome sight. Those on foot could enter as they liked, and did so. They rushed to the gate, cut through

the bars holding it and knocked it down. They did the same with the barriers outside, meeting no resistance. It was all done so quickly that the people in the town were taken unawares. The Prince, the Duke of Lancaster, the Earl of Cambridge, Sir Guichard d'Angle, with all the others and their men burst into the city, followed by pillagers on foot, all in a mood to wreak havoc and do murder, killing indiscriminately for those were their orders. There were pitiful scenes. Men, women and children flung themselves on their knees before the Prince, crying: 'Have mercy on us, gentle Sir!' But he was so inflamed by anger that he would not listen . . . There is no man so hard-hearted that, if he had been in Limoges that day, and had remembered God, he would not have wept bitterly at the fearful slaughter which took place. More than three thousand persons, men, women and children, were dragged out to have their throats cut. May God receive their souls for they were true martyrs.

That the Black Prince commanded this war crime, having been so sensitive to the obligations of chivalry in his earlier years, was due perhaps to the stress of the unravelling of all his victories, coupled with his debilitating illness. In 1371, too sick to cope any longer with the responsibility for English rule in Aquitaine, he returned to England.

The French reconquests continued in 1372. Poitiers opened its gates to du Guesclin. So did **La Rochelle** (see feature), after the Castilian navy defeated an English fleet just off the coast there. Nearby, du Guesclin recaptured his old enemy the Captal of Buch.

In despair at the collapse of their conquests over the preceding 30 years, Edward III and the gravely ill Black Prince made one last effort to campaign personally, when they set sail with an expeditionary force from Sandwich in Kent in 1372. After six weeks at sea, their fleet was driven back to England by incessant storms. They did not attempt a further voyage. Edward III is said to have exclaimed: 'God and St George help us. There was never so evil a King in France as there is now nor ever one who gave me such trouble.'

In 1373 John of Gaunt mounted a further expedition, at the head of 10,000 troops. He landed at Calais and marched, wreaking destruction, through Picardy and Champagne into Burgundy. From there he could have turned towards Paris but chose instead to make a winter crossing through the mountains of the Auvergne to fight in Aquitaine. He

LA ROCHELLE

La Rochelle is a Atlantic fishing port whose harbour is guarded by three imposing medieval towers. The Tour de la Lanterne, built in the fifteenth century, is the most recent. Its fortified, spired roof offers a fine view of the whole port. The two older towers, the Tour Saint Nicolas and the Tour de la Chaine, have a history linking back to the eviction of the English from the city during the Hundred Years War.

La Rochelle once had a citadel, the Château Vauclerc, originally built by Henry II of England, and it was here that an English garrison resided after La Rochelle was transferred, somewhat against its will, to Edward III under the Treaty of Brétigny. In 1372, after the defeat of an English naval force carrying pay for the English troops, the townspeople saw their chance to switch allegiance to the French king, Charles V.

According to the story recounted by Froissart, the mayor of La Rochelle tricked the illiterate English captain into bringing his forces out into the open by reading him a fake letter from Edward III, supposedly requesting a troop inspection and promising that the mayor would pay their wages. The locals then ambushed the English garrison, welcomed in Bertrand du Guesclin and destroyed the château as a symbol of English occupation. They petitioned Charles V never again to allow the building of a citadel that the English could use against them. The two harbour towers, and a third that no longer stands, were then built to celebrate La Rochelle's alliance with the French king.

A display in the Tour de la Chaine tells the subsequent history of the city. Relations with the French monarchy deteriorated during the Wars of Religion, when La Rochelle was staunchly Protestant. The city suffered a terrible siege by Richelieu in 1627–28.

La Rochelle is full of historical interest for the visitor today. As well as seeing the port, you should wander round the old town behind the half-gothic half-eighteenth century Porte de la Grosse Horloge. Many of the streets are arcaded, their thick columns crooked and bow-legged with age, and this gives the whole quarter a unified character.

Particular buildings of note include the High Renaissance Maison Henri II; the idiosyncratic seventeenth-century Maison Venette, a doctor's house decorated with statues of physicians through the ages; the eighteenth-century Hôtel de la Bourse and Palais de Justice; the classic nineteenth-century Café de la Paix; the half-timbered medieval buildings in the rue des Merciers; and the richly decorated Renaissance Hôtel de Ville which has a strikingly elegant stairway inside its courtyard.

The pleasures of La Rochelle are by no means all historical. The market, especially the fish stalls, is splendid. You can visit the new Aquarium, which offers a fine view back across the port and the town, and inspect the yachts and catamarans moored in the nearby docks. You can rent one of La Rochelle's trademark yellow bicycles. You can enjoy the almost-Mediterranean cafés and restaurants around the harbour quays, where enterprising street entertainers perform after dark.

The mood has changed since 1372 and La Rochelle now welcomes the English. They have even taken to calling the road in from the Loire, the D938, the 'Route des Rois d'Angleterre'.

reached Bordeaux with only 6,000 troops, starving and exhausted, the rest having been lost en route. It was a daring raid but he defeated no French armies, captured no French strongholds nor reversed England's continuing loss of her French territories.

The French made a series of advances in Normandy and Brittany, they repossessed Ponthieu and by 1374 had made such inroads into English Aquitaine that it was no larger than when Edward III had first gone to war. England's appetite for conflict was now waning. Edward III was in his dotage and the Black Prince was an invalid. John of Gaunt, though an increasingly dominant figure in English politics, was not a particularly gifted general. Nor was he primarily preoccupied with the French war. In 1372, following the death of his first wife, he had married the daughter of Pedro the Cruel and he now had aspirations to depose Henry of Trastamara and to make himself king of Castile.

On the French side, Charles V's health, never good, was deteriorating. Du Guesclin sensed that France might have reached the limits of what could be achieved militarily at this point. The English remained firmly entrenched in the coastal strip of Aquitaine and Calais and the Duke of Brittany had reverted to his English allegiance – so it was not practical, in the immediate future, to evict the English completely from France.

In 1374 John of Gaunt and du Guesclin therefore concluded a truce in Aquitaine. The following year, with a papal peace initiative in the offing, this truce was extended to cover all of France. From 1375 to 1377 a peace conference deliberated at Bruges. A territorial partition was agreed for Aquitaine, leaving the English with the coastal area centred on Bordeaux. The French retained Ponthieu, while the English kept Calais. However, Charles V was adamant about maintaining his claim to French sovereignty over English Aquitaine – so the underlying issue remained unresolved and the truce remained temporary.

Exit the Cast

During the course of the peace conference, in 1376, the Black Prince died. He was 'deeply mourned for his noble qualities' in England, Froissart records, and shown royal respect in France: 'As soon as the

King of France was informed of the death of his cousin the Prince of Wales, he had his obsequies performed with great solemnity in the Sainte Chapelle in Paris. They were attended by his brothers and by many of the principal French barons and knights. And the King of France maintained that the Prince had ruled his domains nobly and worthily.'

The death of his heir focused Edward III's mind on the English succession (see Chart overleaf). The Black Prince's eldest son had predeceased him. His second son, Richard of Bordeaux, Edward III's young grandson, was next in direct line. Edward III made it quite clear to Parliament and to the country as a whole that Richard, though still a boy, was to be England's next king. That ruled out the crown passing to Edward III's next surviving son (and Richard's uncle), John of Gaunt.

Historians have recently discovered that Edward III also considered the longer term succession issue that could arise a generation later, should Richard die without an obvious heir. He was quite explicit in ruling out succession through the female line of his daughter, Isabella, who had married into the French nobility, or his granddaughter, Philippa. While this is ironic, in view of Edward's own claim to the French throne through his mother's line, he could clearly see the importance of protecting England from the kind of disputes that had so weakened France (and that, indeed, ultimately afflicted England in the fifteenth-century Wars of the Roses).

In 1377 Edward III himself died. Charles V of France had a requiem held for him in Paris, as he had done for the Black Prince. Meanwhile, however, the Bruges truce having expired, Jean de Vienne's French fleet raided the English south coast. The French sacked Rye, attacked Lewes and Plymouth and, on a subsequent expedition, threatened Hastings. In 1380 raids on Winchelsea and Gravesend followed.

However, the English fought back. John Neville of Raby campaigned successfully against French forces in Aquitaine. In Brittany John of Montfort had reverted to allegiance to England. Charles V's ill-judged attempt to impeach him backfired: Montfort repossessed most of western Brittany and gave the port of Brest to England. Charles the Bad also sold the English Cherbourg. Edward III's youngest son,

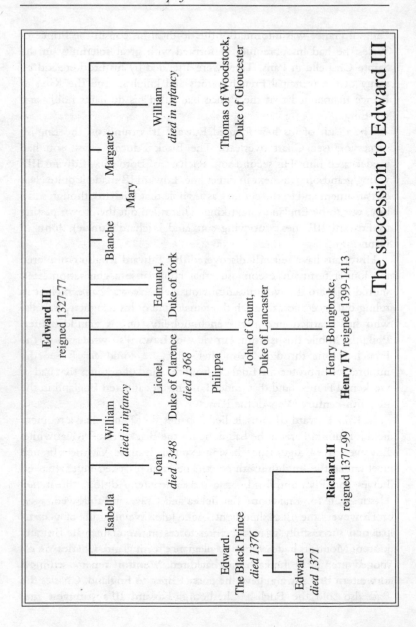

The succession to Edward III

Edward III
reigned 1327-77

Isabella

William
died in infancy

Joan
died 1348

Edward.
The Black Prince
died 1376

Edward
died 1371

Richard II
reigned 1377-99

Lionel,
Duke of Clarence
died 1368

Philippa

John of Gaunt,
Duke of Lancaster

Henry Bolingbroke,
Henry IV reigned 1399-1413

Edmund,
Duke of York

Blanche

Mary

Margaret

William
died in infancy

Thomas of Woodstock,
Duke of Gloucester

Thomas of Woodstock, Earl of Buckingham and later Duke of Gloucester, led a fresh English invasion force south from Calais, burning and destroying as his father and elder brothers had done before him.

In 1380 Bertrand du Guesclin died, besieging a castle in the Auvergne. While he had had his share of defeats as well as victories, he had presided over France's remarkable recovery from the low point of John the Good's captivity. As the funeral cortège made its way slowly north through France, his death was widely mourned – and Charles V knew how much he owed to this loyal, committed general. Du Guesclin had requested that he be buried alongside his wife in Dinan and, indeed, that is where his heart was interred. However, Charles V commanded that his body be entombed alongside France's kings at **Saint-Denis** (see feature), just outside Paris.

A few months later, Charles V also died. In an attempt to secure peace after the recent French reversals, he had offered his daughter in marriage to the young Richard II, with the county of Angoulême for her dowry, but the talks broke down. So Charles died, leaving the two countries still at war. He too had a young heir: his son, Charles VI, now aged 12 – about a year younger than the boy king of England.

The Boy Kings and their Uncles

King Richard II of England grew up to be very different from his warlike father and grandfather. For a start, although born in Bordeaux, he was less French. Indeed he has been described as 'the first King of England since the Norman Conquest to speak fluent English'. He was not by temperament a military commander. He developed interests in literature, art, fashion, fine cuisine and ceremony.

In his boyhood two of his uncles, the Black Prince's younger brothers, were the main powers behind the throne. John of Gaunt, Duke of Lancaster, was the richest and grandest magnate in the country, though increasingly preoccupied with Castile. Thomas of Woodstock, later Duke of Gloucester, was to remain strongly committed to pursuing the war against France.

At the age of 14 Richard faced his first major domestic crisis, the

ST-DENIS

Saint-Denis, just north of Paris, is only a short distance from the famous Parisian hilltop of Montmartre, so-called because a martyr was beheaded on the *mont* there. The martyr was Saint-Denis. According to legend, he picked up his head in his hands and walked north and, where he finally fell, an abbey was founded to commemorate him.

The abbey was demolished and rebuilt more than once before becoming the gothic cathedral, or basilica, of Saint-Denis in which the kings and queens of France were buried. Their tombs and effigies stand in the cathedral's transepts, ambulatory and crypt – and they constitute a remarkable pageant of French history.

The town of Saint-Denis that grew up here is today a noisy, sprawling industrial suburb, criss-crossed by auto-routes, railways and a canal. It is not an attractive setting but the cathedral visit is a 'must' for both architectural and historical interest.

The west front has a fine carving of the Last Judgement, with Christ's outstretched arms, extended by two scrolls to look almost like wings, embracing the scene. This, as with much of the cathedral's design, was commissioned by the twelfth-century Abbot Suger. Further work in the thirteenth-century, including the building of the only tower, and some nineteenth-century restoration by Viollet-le-Duc, completed the building we see today.

The tombs and effigies date from the thirteenth-century onwards but they commemorate kings and queens going back to Clovis (481–511) and the Merovingian dynasty. Beside the altar a thirteenth-century monument to Dagobert (629–39) depicts an elaborate and very lively dream. If you want to walk through the history of France, you can then see the Carolingians, the Capetians and the Valois. The splendid Renaissance mausoleums contrast the monarchs in all their royal finery with their naked corpses. The Bourbon tombs are in the crypt. During the

French Revolution the cathedral was sacked and the bodies exhumed and buried in a ditch. Saint-Denis was temporarily renamed Franciade. However, the tombs were stored safely and in the nineteenth-century tombs and bones were returned to Saint-Denis, with the addition of a memorial to the guillotined Louis XVI and Marie Antoinette. Louis-Philippe's visit to the cathedral in 1837 is portrayed in stained glass above the south transept.

As for the Hundred Years War, almost the whole French cast is here. Philip VI and John the Good, the two most disaster-prone kings of the fourteenth-century, lie side by side in the north transept. Charles V, the Wise, lies beside his queen in the south transept, with Bertrand du Guesclin next to him. The mad Charles VI and his promiscuous queen, Isabeau, lie behind them, while a bust of Charles VII looks out from above. A plaque on the cathedral west front records that Joan of Arc, having been wounded attacking Paris, placed her armour here as an offering to Saint-Denis on 13 September 1429.

The town of Saint-Denis does have one more claim to fame. It is the site of the Stade de France, the nation's famous football stadium, which also offers tourist visits. This is a good 20 minutes' walk from the cathedral and involves crossing over the bus station and under the autoroute flyover. However, the local Office for Cultural Action has erected steel plaques marking all the points of local history, such as where the gas works were constructed in 1889, to sustain your interest en route.

1381 Peasants' Revolt, prompted at least in part by the poll tax imposed to help pay for the war. The rebels burned John of Gaunt's palace, stormed the Tower of London, beheaded the Lord Chancellor and the Treasurer, and burst into the Queen Mother's bedchamber. Richard met them personally, was conciliatory, kept his nerve and then, after the Mayor of London had killed the rebel leader, Wat Tyler, withdrew his concessions and presided over the revolt's suppression.

Throughout his reign Richard was to remain preoccupied with asserting his royal authority at home. Though he continued to style himself king of France, he was ambivalent about taking military action to assert the claim.

Charles VI also had uncles surrounding him, the most influential of whom was Philip, Duke of Burgundy. This was the brave lad nick-named Philip the Bold who had been captured fighting alongside his father, John the Good, at the Battle of Poitiers back in 1356.

In 1382 Philip the Bold invaded Flanders to suppress a rebellion in Ghent, threatening English economic interests there and stimulating an English expeditionary force led by the Bishop of Norwich. The bishop was ignominiously defeated and, on his return to England, impeached.

As a result of the war in Flanders, the French court moved to Amiens and it was here, in 1385, that the young Charles VI met and married the highly sexed Bavarian princess, Isabella, or Isabeau as she came to be called, whom Philip the Bold selected to be France's queen. It was lust at first sight.

That same summer Jean de Vienne led a small force to Scotland to join an attack across the English border. But Philip the Bold dangled in front of his newly wed nephew a much grander design – a full-scale invasion of England: 'You are the greatest King living with the greatest number of subjects and it has occurred to me many times why we do not make this passage to England to crush the great pride of these English ... and make this great enterprise one of eternal memory.' When, in 1386, John of Gaunt left England with 200 ships to try and enforce his claim to the throne of Castile, France's best opportunity arrived.

The preparations were on a huge scale. At Sluys, in the Low Countries, an army of 30,000 men and a fleet of 1,200 ships assembled.

Supplies were requisitioned from all over north-west France: swords, lances, armour, catapults, cannonballs, arrows, wheat, smoked and dried fish, cattle, sheep, hens, cheese, wine, timber, straw, ropes, horses and carts. These were preparations, Froissart tells us, 'the like of which were never known in the memory of man or recorded history. Money was no more spared than if it had rained from the skies or been drawn up from the sea.'

Amazingly, anticipating the artificial Mulberry harbour towed across the Channel in the other direction for the 1944 Normandy landings, the French constructed a portable wooden fortress, which they intended to transport. It had a high wooden wall and towers that had been prefabricated so that they could be packed and shipped in numbered sections. The idea was that, once it had been unpacked on the English coast, it could be assembled in a few hours and would protect all the houses, barracks, stables and stalls that the French would need to sustain 30,000 troops in their bridgehead over a long period.

French intentions were, of course, known in England. Although extra prayers were said, and some panic ensued, Froissart records another reaction: 'Let the Frenchmen come. Not a man jack of them will ever get back to France.'

Given the practicalities of invading an English kingdom very much more coherently organized and equipped to defend itself than the Anglo-Saxon monarchy William the Conqueror had attacked in 1066, perhaps it is not surprising that the French fleet never set sail. First, over the summer of 1386, they waited for the royal leaders. Charles VI, who was keen, arrived with the Duke of Burgundy and a second royal uncle. But the third royal uncle, the Duke of Berry, tarried. Then the winds were unfavourable. As autumn gave way to winter, the admirals became gloomier. Finally, Froissart quotes the Duke of Berry saying to the Duke of Burgundy:

> Dear brother, I cannot deny that I have been present in France at most of the councils at which this expedition has been decided upon, but I have since given much thought to these problems, for they concern a greater and more important undertaking than any that a King of France has attempted before. In view of everything, and considering the dangers and unexpected consequences that could damage the kingdom of France, I should not dare

to advise that we should send the king to sea as late in the year as December, when the sea is cold and hostile.

While the uncles decided to postpone the invasion until the following summer, it did not happen then either. These uncles were the sons of John the Good. They remembered what it had been like to have the King of France in English captivity and how serious the consequences had nearly been. As the Duke of Berry said:

> Even supposing we made ... a landing, it is a sea-girt country which presents serious hazards for the conduct of a military campaign, with the risk that our fleet and all our provisions could be destroyed in a single night, for we cannot defend ourselves on both sea and land. If it turned out that we were beaten and the king slain or captured, the kingdom of France would be lost to us without hope of recovery, since the whole flower of our knighthood is here.

While Charles VI felt some frustration with the rule of his uncles, Richard II had a much more serious problem. With John of Gaunt still away in France, the Black Prince's youngest brother, the violently anti-French Duke of Gloucester, became a major force in English politics and led a baronial revolt against the unpopular favourites with whom Richard II had surrounded himself. Richard accused his uncle of behaving treasonably and threatened to seek assistance from France. Given that the French had just been planning to invade England, this was a rash, as well as a tactless, move. Gloucester reminded Richard II pointedly of the fate of his royal great-grandfather, Edward II, who had been deposed from the throne and then murdered. Gloucester and his main ally, the Earl of Arundel, renewed English naval attacks on the French.

In 1387 Richard II defiantly appointed a council from among his favourites. It was short-lived. After some brief armed conflict, Gloucester and four other barons – the earls of Arundel, Warwick, Nottingham and Derby (this last was Henry Bolingbroke, John of Gaunt's son and heir) – secured parliamentary backing to execute or outlaw Richard's favourites. Against these favourites the nobles brought various charges, including neglecting the defence of the kingdom and inducing the king to treat with France. Richard's dignity was respected, but his authority was not.

The Boy Kings come of Age

In 1388, now aged 20, Charles VI of France dismissed his uncles and assumed power himself. He was probably urged on to this course by his younger brother, Louis, Duke of Orléans, and by Queen Isabeau. Charles VI appointed his own councillors, some of whom had previously served his father, and they were mainly interested in domestic reform and in peace.

In 1389 Richard II, aged 22, announced that, with the mistakes of his early years behind him, he too would take the reins of government into his own hands and John of Gaunt returned from Spain to support him. England's recent military initiatives having achieved little, Richard judged he could now negotiate a truce with the French. This was signed at Leulinghen, near Calais. Though Gloucester remained a die-hard opponent, both countries were interested in exploring the possibility of a settled peace.

In 1392 Charles VI went mad. He was leading a march through a forest near Le Mans on a hot summer's day, when a barefoot lunatic grasped his bridle and shouted at him to go no further for he was 'betrayed'. When the king and his companions later emerged from the forest into the blinding sunlight, and an escort accidentally dropped a lance with a sudden clang, Charles VI, startled, shouted 'Forward against the traitors' and began attacking his own followers. After rushing wildly round, he finally fell down in a daze, exhausted, and was taken back to Paris. He recovered but continued thereafter to have intermittent fits of madness. He also spent much of his time pursuing frivolous pleasures, including attending a masked ball at which a number of the guests were burned to death. While a long reign still lay ahead of him, he no longer directed French policy.

Richard II, meanwhile, continued to pursue peace. He surrendered Cherbourg and Brest, in 1393 and 1396 respectively. He signalled some flexibility about the issue of homage for Aquitaine (whose duke was now John of Gaunt), though not enough to reach full agreement with

France on the issue. Then in 1395, following the death of his first wife the previous year, he took a decisive step to bring the Anglo-French conflict to an end: he sent ambassadors to France to propose marriage to Charles VI's daughter, Isabella. That Charles was his own contemporary, and Charles's daughter aged six, did not deter him. Their marriage took place by proxy in Paris in 1396.

Richard II then went to France to meet Charles VI, his new father-in-law, near Calais. While no full diplomatic settlement was possible – given the unresolved dispute about homage for Aquitaine and the continuing English occupation of Calais – it was agreed to extend the truce for 28 years. The aim was to bury half a century of Anglo-French hostility and allow the next generation to grow up in a new relationship of peace.

It was Richard II who brought about this Anglo-French reconciliation. It was Richard II who, unintentionally, then swiftly destroyed it. He became increasingly arrogant and imperious, and he scorned the need to build support among the leading nobles of the realm. Revealingly, he asked the Pope to canonize the deposed and murdered Edward II. In 1397 Richard took his revenge on the barons who had humiliated him ten years earlier. He had the Earl of Arundel arrested and beheaded. He condemned the Earl of Warwick to death, then softened his sentence to banishment. He imprisoned his uncle, the Duke of Gloucester, in Calais and had him murdered there. After a quarrel over allegations of a plot between Thomas Mowbray, previously Earl of Nottingham and now Duke of Norfolk, and John of Gaunt's son, Henry Bolingbroke, Richard II intervened to halt a duel and banished Mowbray for life and Bolingbroke for ten years.

In 1399 John of Gaunt, Duke of Lancaster – Richard II's uncle and, certainly in later years, his loyal ally – died. The duchy of Lancaster carried huge estates, making its duke England's greatest baronial landowner. The new Duke of Lancaster was now Henry Bolingbroke, Richard II's cousin and, like Richard (who had no children), a direct male descendant from Edward III. Richard prolonged Bolingbroke's banishment to a life sentence and confiscated his Lancastrian estates.

Bolingbroke invaded England, swiftly won widespread support, unseated Richard II from the throne in an enforced abdication, and in October 1399 was himself crowned King Henry IV of England. Richard II died mysteriously in captivity a few months later and Henry sent Richard's young French queen, Isabella, back to France.

CHAPTER FIVE

The Lancastrian Reconquest

The Lancastrian Achievement

In the fifteenth century the Lancastrian kings of England finally won the French throne and, for a period, the king of England actually was the king of France. After a military interlude during Henry IV's reign, and following Henry V's famous victories, the third of the Lancastrians, King Henry VI of England, became 'Henri II, roi de France'. Not everyone in France agreed, of course, and fighting continued – but for a period England and France were governed in the name of an Anglo-French dual monarchy.

Although he had defeated and imprisoned a French king, the first 'English king of France', Edward III, had never come close to gaining the French throne himself. His heir, Richard II, had not even been able to keep his English title. The Lancastrian achievement was not only to win the French crown but also, albeit insecurely and incompletely, to govern France. How did such a dramatic resurgence of English military strength become possible?

Madness in France

The Lancastrian opportunity arose from the disintegration of France into warring factions. The French king, Charles VI, slipped in and out of madness. At times he thought himself made of glass, liable to be shattered, and lashed out with his sword at anyone who came near him. At other times he howled like a wolf. At the heart of the French government, therefore, was a power vacuum, which two rivals contended to fill.

The first was Louis, Duke of Orléans, the king's brother and, it was said, the lover of the French queen, Isabeau. He was no friend of England. Appalled at Richard II's deposition and subsequent death, he was also indignant at the humiliating treatment Richard's French child widow, Isabella, had received at the hands of the first of the Lancastrians, Henry IV: 'How could you suffer my much redoubted lady the Queen of England to return so desolate to this country after the death of her lord, despoiled by your rigour and cruelty of her dower, which you detain from her and likewise the portion she carried here on her marriage.'

Henry IV denied he had robbed Richard II's queen before dispatching her back to France, but peace between the two kingdoms was at an end. The Duke of Orléans led an attack on English territory in Aquitaine. To finance this and other expansionist ambitions he imposed taxes which made him unpopular and vulnerable in the contest for power in France.

His rival was Philip the Bold, Duke of Burgundy and uncle to both Charles VI and Louis of Orléans. Burgundy, though in theory owing allegiance to the king of France, was, in size and power, in effect a rival kingdom. Because it was subsequently absorbed into France, it is difficult now to imagine but there was almost another country in between a much smaller France and the Holy Roman Empire. Its territory included Flanders, one of the richest and most prosperous parts of Europe, together with Artois and Burgundy itself. Its income was enhanced by taxes collected nominally on behalf of the French king, but never passed on. It had a rich court life of its own, with its capital at **Dijon** (see feature) and, by medieval standards, a fully-fledged government. In the early fifteenth century Philip the Bold was arguably the foremost ruler in Christendom.

The Duke of Burgundy's priorities were to consolidate and secure his own territories. So the Burgundian 'foreign policy' was very different from the Orléanist. The Burgundian and Orléanist factions were pulling France in opposite directions.

In 1404 Philip the Bold died and was succeeded by his son, John. In

DIJON

Dijon, capital of the dukes of Burgundy and thus the capital of a major European power in the fourteenth and fifteenth centuries, still retains a certain majesty today. Its towers, its extensive public buildings, its Arc de Triomphe and the line of gaudy flags that flank the approach to the ducal palace lift it above the status of a French provincial city.

The ducal palace is Dijon's principal attraction to visitors. While much of the medieval structure has disappeared and been incorporated piecemeal into a later classical design, the view from the place des Ducs de Bourgogne of a gothic façade topped by a 150 foot tower evokes the era of the Hundred Years War. Inside a courtyard stand an older tower built by Philip the Bold and the Chapter House surviving from a destroyed chapel. The vast ducal kitchens, which date from 1435, convey an impression of the scale of the feasts that characterized medieval ducal life.

The palace now houses Dijon's Museum of Fine Arts, which, in several respects, vividly portrays the richness and splendour of medieval Burgundy. A fine selection of Flemish and Burgundian paintings and a magnificent crucifixion altarpiece, originally from the ducal mausoleum at the Charterhouse of Champnol, now reside here. A portrait of the fifteenth-century duke, Philip the Good, by Rogier van der Weyden's workshop, shows him wearing the decoration of the Order of the Golden Fleece (which he founded). Beside it stands the tomb of Philip the Bold, carved between 1385 and 1410 by Claus Suter among others. Philip's effigy lies on a black marble slab with two angels at his head and a lion at his feet. In alabaster niches below the slab some 40 sculpted mourners grieve his death. Nearby lies the similarly-styled double tomb of John the Fearless and Margaret of Bavaria, with four angels, two lions and another 40 mourners.

The area immediately to the north and west of the ducal palace, much of it now pedestrianized, still preserves a medieval character. Half-timbered houses and shops are a prominent feature of the rue Verrerie, the rue de la Chouette and the rue des Forges. The distinctive Burgundian multi-coloured tiled roofs can be glimpsed between towers and spires. The thirteenth-century church of Notre-Dame has an extraordinarily well-preserved gothic façade with arcaded galleries and three tiers of gargoyles. Its Jacquemart clock was brought from Flanders by Philip the Bold after a military victory. Jacquemart is the name given to the figure who strikes the clock bell. Over the centuries the people of Dijon have given him a wife (in 1610), a son called Jacquelinet (in 1714) and a daughter, Jacquelinette (in 1881).

Other places to visit in the city include the cathedral, with a Romanesque crypt and rotunda; the law courts, formerly the Burgundian parlement; and a fine nineteenth-century blue and white iron market hall with orange brickwork and matching orange awnings.

To the south of the city, at the start of the route des Grands Crus through Burgundy's most famous vineyards in the old village of Chenove, lie the wine cellars of the medieval dukes of Burgundy. A wide wooden-roofed fifteenth-century building houses two enormous thirteenth-century wine presses, capable of pressing 100 casks of wine at a time, which also conveys something about the scale of the ducal feasts.

A few miles further south is the remarkable Hôtel Dieu at Beaune, a medieval hospital founded by the fifteenth-century Burgundian chancellor, Nicolas Rolin.

1396 John had led a French crusade to help the Hungarians keep the Ottoman Turks at bay. He had been captured and the expedition was a failure but it did earn him the nickname of John the Fearless. John was harsh, crafty and a dangerous enemy.

He swiftly clashed with Louis of Orléans in the French Council. Their respective supporters fought in the streets. When the Orléanists adopted the emblem of a wooden club, the Burgundians chose the symbol of a carpenter's plane to emphasize their superior strength.

On a winter night in 1407 Louis, Duke of Orléans was returning through the streets of Paris from a visit to the queen when he was ambushed. He and a few attendants were tricked into a street near the Porte Barbette where 18 armed men were waiting for them in the shadows. According to the contemporary chronicler Enguerrand de Monstrelet:

> As the duke approached the gate they leapt upon him in a wild fury, and one of them shouted; 'Kill him!' dealing him a blow with his axe which severed his hand clean at the wrist.
>
> The duke, seeing such a cruel attack made upon him, shouted out loud: 'I am the Duc d'Orléans', to which some of those who were striking at him answered: 'That's just what we wanted to know'. At this the rest of the men joined in, and shortly the duke was knocked off his mule and his head so smashed with blows that the brains ran out on the roadway. Even then they turned him over and over, so hacking at him that he was very soon completely dead.

John the Fearless wept at the Duke of Orléans's funeral but, when the French Council launched an investigation into the murder, he boasted 'Know you that by my orders was the Duke of Orléans killed'.

In the aftermath of this event France descended into civil war. John the Fearless attempted to justify the murder by documenting Louis's peculation and debauchery. He also courted the support of the Paris bourgeoisie, identifying himself with their bid to reduce the burden of royal taxation.

The Orléanist leadership passed to Bernard, Count of Armagnac, whose daughter married Louis's son, the young Charles of Orléans. When Armagnac forces attempted to blockade Paris in 1411, John the Fearless appealed to Henry IV for aid, offering help in the conquest of

Normandy in return. A small English force landed at Calais, relieving the pressure on Paris but not conquering any French territory.

The following year the Armagnac party sought English aid, offering territorial concessions in Aquitaine. Again an English force landed, led by the Duke of Clarence, one of Henry IV's younger sons, and eventually it had to be paid handsomely to leave. Here – in the interplay between French civil strife, English opportunity for profit, and the dormant English claim to French territory – lay the seeds of the next phase of the Hundred Years War. All that was needed was a new English leader.

Henry V goes to War

Although Henry IV had assumed the title of king of France, he was far too busy defending what many saw as his usurpation of the English crown against plots and rebellions at home to have time for overseas conquests. In 1413, having been ill from what was thought to be leprosy, he died.

He was succeeded by his son, Henry V, now aged 25. Henry V's portrait shows him with a pudding-basin haircut, a long nose, and a cold puritanical look. His father's domestic rebellions had provided him with a military training. At the age of 16 he had led one flank of his father's army in battle and then played a prominent part in suppressing a prolonged rebellion (supported by the French) in Wales. Thus he grew up as a military commander and learned the techniques of siege warfare, which he would in due course fully apply in France. He also developed a streak of ruthlessness, not to say cruelty. The story is often told of how he superintended the burning of the Lollard heretic, John Badby in 1409. When Badby began to scream, Henry pulled him from the flames and invited him to recant. When Badby declined, Henry thrust him back into the fire.

If in his youth Henry V had indeed led the madcap life with his drinking companions portrayed by Shakespeare, he came to the throne with serious ambitions. He had acted as President of the Council during his father's illness and at one point had reportedly demanded that his father abdicate in his favour. One of his first acts was to establish English as the language of English royal administration. In foreign policy he had opposed the English expedition his father had sent to assist the Armagnac cause and favoured an alliance with Burgundy. As an experienced military leader, he probably had ambitions to invade France from the outset of his reign.

Meanwhile John the Fearless had incited the Parisian mob, led by the butcher Simon Caboche, to invade the royal palace and to slaughter Armagnac supporters in the streets. The more moderate Parisian burghers were appalled and in 1413 called on the Armagnacs to make another attempt to drive the Burgundians out of the capital. This time, led by the Dauphin Louis, the Armagnac forces succeeded. After an abortive attempt to kidnap the mad King Charles VI, John the Fearless fled Paris and returned to Burgundy.

Henry V opened negotiations with John the Fearless and offered to support him against the Armagnacs provided the Duke did not oppose his claim to be king of France. Next he laid out his demands to the French royal house. He reasserted his title to their throne, then demanded the whole of the former English territories in France, plus Normandy, part of Provence, the unpaid portion of John II's ransom and the hand in marriage of Charles VI's daughter, Catherine (sister of the now-deceased Isabella who had been Richard II's queen).

Not surprisingly, the French gave Henry a defiant answer: 'With regard to those things you claim, you have no right, not even to the Throne of England, which belongs to the true heirs of the late King Richard. Nor are you a man with which our King can safely treat.'

So Henry began to assemble an invasion force. He had already secured the necessary finance. Parliament had voted him a subsidy in 1414 and this was topped up by loans, including one of £2,000 from the rich London merchant, Dick Whittington. Although in theory the King still had the right to call up a feudal army, in practice military service was now a professional business. Soldiers were contracted and were paid on a scale determined by rank. Dukes were paid thirteen shillings and fourpence a day, earls six shillings and eightpence, barons four shillings, knights two shillings, other men-at-arms one shilling and archers sixpence. Plunder and ransom also formed part of the reward.

Henry raised an army of about 10,000 – composed of 8,000 archers

Amiens cathedral
Photo Ville d'Amiens – Bernard Maison

Château-Gaillard

The castle at
St-Saveur-le-Vicomte

Caen castle

Site of the battle of Crécy
Comité du Tourisme de la Somme

Rodin's statue of the six burghers
of Calais

Bordeaux's summer wine festival

The 'bastide' of Bassoues in the Gers

OPPOSITE PAGE

Carcassone

The abbey of Nouaille–Maupertuis, near the battlefield of Poitiers

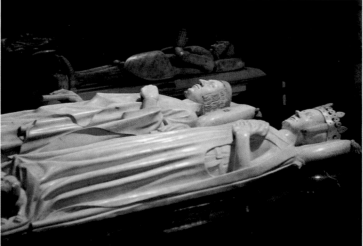

La Rochelle harbour fortifications

The tomb of Philip the Bold at Dijon

OPPOSITE PAGE

The old town of Dinan

The tombs of Charles V and his queen at St-Denis

The church of St Jean in Troyes

The market place in Rouen

OPPOSITE PAGE

The modern museum at Agincourt

Falaise castle

The house of Jacques Coeur in Bourges

The River Loire at Orléans

OPPOSITE PAGE

Joan of Arc's village church at Domrémy

Statue of Joan of Arc in front of Reims cathedral

OPPOSITE PAGE
The château of Chinon

The Grand' Place at Arras

Fougères

OPPOSITE PAGE
Tours cathedral

The château of Castelnaud

Medieval weaponry at Castelnaud

Tickets for the re-enactment of the battle of Castillon

The real battlefield at Castillon-de-Bataille

and 2,000 men–at–arms – supported by fearsome (but not very reliable) cannon with names such as 'the King's Daughter', 'London' and 'Messenger'. The troops gathered in the Portsmouth-Southampton area, practising their skills and waiting to embark.

The logistics of an invasion were complex and Henry supervised them personally from Portchester Castle. Some 1,500 ships were hired or commandeered. The flagship was the 500-ton *Trinity Royal*, with a crew of 300, but ships as small as 20 tons helped make up the fleet. Over 10,000 horses and pack animals were taken for transport, together with herds of cattle to be butchered for meat. Siege engineers, miners, masons, shoemakers, chaplains, musicians and cooks made up a substantial auxiliary support.

Harfleur and Agincourt

Leaving his brother John, Duke of Bedford in charge in England, Henry V set sail with his invasion force on 11 August 1415. Three days later he landed near Harfleur, in Normandy, near the mouth of the Seine (Le Havre did not exist at the time). The first man to leap ashore was Sir John Fastolf (later immortalized by Shakespeare as Falstaff) whom Henry duly rewarded with a house in France.

The destination had been kept strictly secret and the main French forces were elsewhere. But if Henry thought the capture of Harfleur would be easy, he soon learned otherwise. The town was defended by strong walls with 26 towers and a moat. Marshy terrain and deliberately flooded fields made assault difficult. Moreover, just before the English completed a stockade to cut off supplies or assistance to the town, a local nobleman slipped in with 300 extra soldiers.

Henry enforced strict discipline upon his troops. They all had to wear the identification badge of the cross of Saint George. They were not to molest the local women, nor to consort with prostitutes. Looting was forbidden. But despite the single-mindedness of the attackers, and the damage inflicted on the ramparts by the English guns, the defenders showed no sign of defeat.

The siege lasted well into September and by then the English army began to suffer the ravages of dysentery, probably caused by contaminated water. This was a far more serious threat to them than the French. The earls of Arundel and Suffolk and the Bishop of Norwich died from it, as did perhaps as many as 2,000 soldiers. Many more had to be shipped home, too ill to fight.

Finally on 22 September, after the English captured one of the gates, and when it was clear that no French reinforcements would be sent, Harfleur surrendered. But by then Henry V had lost about a third of his army. What could he do next?

His first decision was to colonize Harfleur. Nobles were either sent to England or released on parole to raise their ransoms. Many of the townsfolk were expelled, without their belongings, and their wealth was confiscated. Then advertisements were circulated in England to attract English merchants and artisans to settle there and, in due course, about 10,000 did so. Henry wanted Harfleur, as a strategic port, to become another Calais.

But what to do after that was a dilemma. Henry's army was no longer strong enough to march on Paris or south to Aquitaine, as he probably originally intended. A garrison would have to be left in Harfleur and the remaining 6,000 or so were likely to have to face a French army several times that number if they advanced. Henry challenged the Dauphin Louis to single combat for the throne of France but the Dauphin, a sickly youth who was to die shortly afterwards, wisely declined. The English Council of War advocated returning direct to England.

Henry overruled his advisers, however, and chose to emulate Edward III's march through Normandy to Calais. And, just like his great-grandfather, Henry found it very difficult to cross the Somme. Moreover, the French had reinforced Edward III's old crossing at Blanchetaque near the river mouth. For about a week Henry was therefore driven eastwards along the south side of the Somme, with one French army pursuing him from behind and another one on the north bank of the river harassing him and hampering his efforts to cross. Finally he outpaced his pursuers and found two unguarded fords at Voyennes and Bethencourt. But, although now on the north bank, he was still several days' march away from Calais. The French forces were much closer and had united into an army of about 30,000.

On the night of 24 October the French took up a position blocking the Calais road near the village of **Agincourt** (see feature) while the English camped about a mile away at Maisoncelles, hungry and wet. Henry sent envoys to the French, offering to return Harfleur in exchange for safe passage to Calais. The French, confident of victory in battle the next day, rejected the idea. So Henry prepared his troops to fight. His eve-of-battle words of encouragement were to become the basis of one of Shakespeare's best-known scenes.

On 25 October, the feast of Saint Crispin and Saint Crispianus, the small English army, about 6,000 in number, faced the massed French force, estimated at about five times as many. Henry called on his troops to fight bravely and honourably and warned them that the French had threatened to cut off three fingers from the right hand of each of the archers they captured, to ensure that they were never able to draw a bowstring again.

The location, though chosen by the French, favoured the English. The vast French army had very little room for manoeuvre between the two woods on either side of the battlefield (see Map 11, p. 122). For the much smaller English force, this was less of an issue.

To begin with, neither side made any move. They watched one another for most of the morning. Then, on their king's command, the English archers advanced to within bow-shot range of the French and planted a fence of stakes in front of themselves. Then they opened fire. Constrained by the woods on either side, the French troops were an easy target and the English arrows raining down on them caused havoc, particularly among the horses. Enguerrand de Monstrelet's chronicle records:

> The company under Sir Clugnet de Brabant who were detailed to break the line of the English archers were reduced from eight hundred to seven score before the attempt was made. Sir Guillaume de Saveuses, who was also in this company, rushed ahead of his own men, thinking they would follow him, but before he had dealt many blows among the archers he was pulled from his horse and killed. Most of the others and all their horses were driven back among the vanguard by fear of the English archers, and there they did much damage, breaking the line in several places; so many of the horses were wounded by English arrows that their riders could not control them,

AGINCOURT

Agincourt, spelled Azincourt today, is a small village between Hesdin and Saint-Omer, easily visited en route to or from Calais. You know you are near when you start to be greeted from the hedgerows by a series of brightly painted full-size cardboard cut-out figures of medieval knights, archers and men-at-arms.

The village has cheered up the single-storey buildings so common in northern France with white walls, red-tiled roofs and baskets of geraniums, giving itself almost a southern look. It makes the most of its history. Showing no shame in commemorating his defeat, the local restaurant names itself after the mad King Charles VI.

The museum, run with much enthusiasm by a local couple, makes a good starting point. They have adopted a strong, and commercially shrewd anglophile stance and the most painfully inadequate attempts to speak French are rewarded with praise. In the summer of 2001 they moved into a new building whose facade has been designed with a longbow theme. Inside you learn about the origins of the war, daily life at the time, armies and weapons, the chroniclers, and other background details partly from display panels and partly from talking heads inside television sets on top of costumed models whose voices are only audible, in a choice of languages, through earphones.

Then you go into a series of three audio-visual displays. The first, loosely derived from Shakespeare, is about the eve of battle. The second, the centrepiece of the whole museum, is about the Battle of Agincourt itself and is excellent, using modern technology cleverly without losing clarity. The third includes clips of Henry V feature films but is embarrassingly patriotic in its style of presentation. Upstairs are a couple of videos about the war and techniques of warfare, including interviews with French and English academics, and some 'hands on' displays of weaponry and armour. You can lift swords and maces, for example, and look through a fifteenth-century helmet visor and appreciate just how little the combatants were able to see. Compared to the amateur displays previously available, the new museum represents a substantial investment and has achieved a good mix of adult and child appeal.

Leaving the museum, you will be given a leaflet describing the battlefield circuit of about five kilometres, which you can either walk or drive. You will be ushered round the circuit by a few more cardboard cut-out figures. A monument with a *table d'orientation* makes one obvious stopping point and a crucifix marking a mass French grave makes another.

The museum apparently receives flowers from England on the anniversary of Henry V's death. While it is hard to know for sure what the locals make of all this, it is easy to guess.

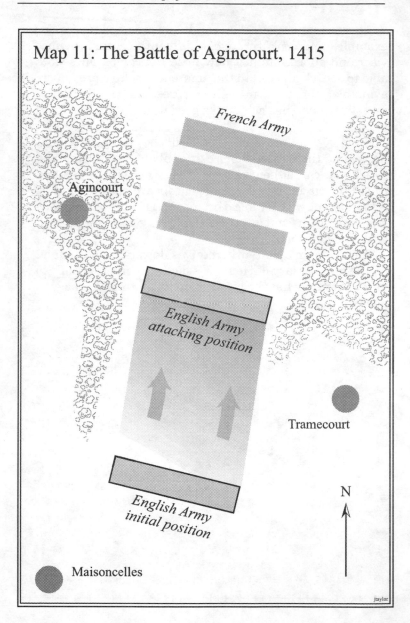

Map 11: The Battle of Agincourt, 1415

and they caused many more knights to fall and so disordered their ranks that some fled behind the enemy in fear of their lives and others were forced to withdraw into some newly sown land. Their example caused many more French from the main body to flee.

The English swiftly followed up their advantage and engaged the main French army in hand-to-hand fighting, inflicting heavy losses and suffering very few of their own. One of the problems the French faced was the sheer weight of their armour. Once they had fallen down, either struck by an English arrow or just through the pressure of their own overcrowded ranks, they found it very difficult to move. The English used their unarmoured archers in the hand-to-hand fighting to great effect. The French killed and wounded became piled on top of one another, and the more mobile English archers clambered over them.

Henry himself fought in the thick of the battle. According to one French chronicler, he had two decoys, dressed like himself and wearing crowns, fighting as well. But that he personally shared the dangers of the troops he was leading is not in doubt. Apart from a dent in his helmet, he remained unhurt. His corpulent cousin, the Duke of York died, but from exhaustion, without having been wounded.

In the muddy chaos that followed the hand-to-hand fighting, the English captured thousands of prisoners. Indeed the number of unarmed French prisoners soon dwarfed the number of their armed English captors and took up much of their attention. So when the prospect of a fresh French attack was reported, Henry V cold-bloodedly ordered the slaughter of the French prisoners. Not only did this order contravene the laws of warfare, it also threatened to deprive the English of a fortune in ransoms. When the English soldiers protested, Henry detailed his own guard to carry out the task. One group of prisoners was burnt to death in a hut but most had their throats cut or were stabbed through the visors of their helmets. In the event the fresh French attack never materialized. The remaining French troops fled.

Henry's tiny army had won the most remarkable of victories. French losses may have numbered as many as 10,000 and the French captives included Charles, Duke of Orléans, the son of the duke murdered by John the Fearless.

Touring the battlefield and taking in the scale of the killing, Henry declared: 'It is not we but God Almighty who has ordered this great slaughter, to punish the French for their sins.' French prisoners waited on the English victors at table that night: the chivalry that had characterized the Black Prince's victory at Poitiers was dead.

With the French defeated, the road to Calais was open. Henry took it and then sailed back to England. London gave him a celebratory welcome, with an extravagant pageant and much dancing in the streets. A chorus of girls sang 'Welcome Henry the Fifte, Kynge of England and of Fraunce'. But was he? As Edward III had found out, individual victories, however spectacular, do not capture crowns.

Ruthless Conquest

Although it is conventional to regard the battles as the main events in wars, the lull between the Agincourt campaign of 1415 and Henry's next invasion of France in 1417 was perhaps the pivotal point in the Hundred Years War. The settlement of Harfleur as an English colony was indicative of the change in English ambitions. Henry was no longer satisfied with capturing prisoners and booty – he was determined to conquer, and keep, French territory.

He made financial, military and diplomatic preparations. In the aftermath of his famous victory he had little trouble securing more money from Parliament. Sheriffs all over England were instructed to pluck goose feathers and send them to London for arrow making. The navy was expanded and in 1416 swiftly defeated an attempted blockade of Harfleur by a combined French-Genoese fleet.

Meanwhile Henry was entertaining the Holy Roman Emperor Sigismund, whose ambition was to unite Europe behind a crusade against the Turks. Henry persuaded him, in the interests of resolving the Anglo-French conflict, to support his own claim to the French crown. He and Sigismund then crossed to Calais and held a secret meeting with John the Fearless, Duke of Burgundy. Henry probably persuaded the Duke to remain neutral in the event of an English invasion of France, in breach of his feudal duty to Charles VI. The exact nature of any agreement is obscure but, on the strength of a draft document, at least one French historian, Joseph Calmette, detected treason:

> John recognized Henry and his descendants as the heirs to the French throne, and solemnly undertook to pay liege homage as soon as Henry had recovered a sizeable share of the kingdom, adding that he was prepared to offer Henry there and then 'all the help he could by secret ways and means'. The document is no more than a draft, but it is *in the duke's handwriting* ... His first crime had been committed with an axe in 1407; the second was committed with the pen in 1417.

In July 1417 Henry V set sail again with an army of about 10,000 and made a surprise landing at the mouth of the River Touques, between the modern beach resorts of Deauville and Trouville. From there he attacked **Caen** (for feature, see Chapter Two), which had been sacked by Edward III in 1346 and which had built itself new stout fortifications as a result.

The citizens of Caen prepared for a siege and quickly identified the two famous abbeys that overlooked their city centre as points of vulnerability. Calculating the potential damage if the abbeys fell into English hands and were used as an artillery base, the Caen defenders decided to make a pre-emptive strike and destroy them. However, a French monk was reportedly so horrified at this prospect that he fled to the English camp and helped the English capture the abbeys.

With the abbeys as his headquarters Henry V turned his guns on Caen and he and his brother, the Duke of Clarence, led an assault into the city streets. While a French garrison continued to defend the castle, the people of Caen were at the mercy of the English. Some 2,000 inhabitants were massacred in and around the marketplace and plundering was widespread. The castle garrison then surrendered. Henry set up the beginnings of a government based in Caen. He offered privileges and tax exemptions to those of its citizens who were willing to acknowledge him as both the rightful duke of Normandy and the rightful king of France. Meanwhile he invited further settlers to come across from England.

After that the English conquest of Normandy proceeded rapidly. Many towns surrendered without resistance. In Lisieux the entire population fled, leaving only two cripples behind. Bayeux, Argentan and Alençon fell. Truces were concluded with Anjou, Maine and Brittany. Apart from some defiant monks in Mont Saint-Michel, that left only the fortified town of **Falaise** (see feature, p. 128–9).

Falaise Castle, on a rocky cliff, withstood the English attack for ten weeks. Henry surrounded the town and bombarded it with gun-stones which were two feet in diameter. The damage to churches, houses and shops was dramatic and, after four weeks, the townsfolk surrendered. But the castle fought on for another six weeks, its stout walls withstanding the artillery pounding. Only when the English started digging away at the castle's foundations did the garrison finally yield.

In the spring of 1418 Henry advanced into Upper Normandy and attacked its principal city, **Rouen** (featured in Chapter Six). In the French civil war Rouen had thrown out its Armagnac garrison and committed itself to support the Burgundian cause. But John the Fearless made no attempt to protect this ally from Henry.

The city council of Rouen had prepared for the English arrival by destroying all the suburbs and farms outside their city walls, so that there was no shelter or sustenance for a besieging army. Any family unable to stock enough food for a lengthy siege was ordered to leave. Henry surrounded the city, kept his troops at a distance, and made no serious attempt to take it by force. Instead he resolved to starve it into submission, however many months it took. He must have been confident that the Duke of Burgundy would not come to the city's rescue.

By winter the people of Rouen had exhausted their food stocks and were close to starvation. They had already consumed their donkeys and horses; now they were eating dogs, cats, and rodents or chewing their shoe leather. In December they decided to expel the women and children, the old and the sick. Some 12,000 'useless mouths' in all were thrust into the 'no-man's land' between their city walls and the English army. As a result of their own earlier scorched-earth policy, there was nothing to eat here. They hoped that Henry would show these weak and harmless refugees compassion and either feed them or, at least, allow them through the English lines into the Norman hinterland where they might fend for themselves. Henry did neither. He ordered that the refugees remain where they were trapped, so that the

Rouennais who had expelled them could watch them die beneath their walls. The English soldier John Page gave a first-hand account of this further example of Henry V's ruthlessness:

> There one might see wandering here and there children of two or three years old begging for bread as their parents were dead. These wretched people had only sodden soil under them and they lay there crying for food – some starving to death, some unable to open their eyes and no longer breathing, others cowering on their knees as thin as twigs. A woman was there clutching her dead child to her breast to warm it, and a child was sucking the breast of its dead mother. There one could easily count ten or twelve dead to one alive...

Finally, in January 1419, reduced virtually to skeletons, the Rouennais capitulated. Henry imposed a large fine on them as a punishment for resisting their rightful ruler.

He then established Rouen as the capital of an English Normandy. Across the province estates were confiscated and given as rewards to the English nobles and captains – provided they stayed in Normandy and provided garrisons or undertook other military duties.

The Duke of Burgundy's Skull

Meanwhile the French royal family had become hopelessly weak and divided. King Charles VI remained intermittently mad but, during one of his bouts of sanity, the Count of Armagnac had reported to him one of Queen Isabeau's love affairs. The lover was tortured, sewn in a sack and thrown in the Seine. Queen Isabeau was exiled to Tours, where she was kept under guard.

Furious and resentful, the Queen wrote to John the Fearless, Duke of Burgundy, begging him to rescue her. He sent 800 horsemen to release her, met her at Chartres and escorted her to **Troyes** (see feature, p. 130–1) where he established her as regent. Here Isabeau set up her own court, styling herself 'Queen of France, having on behalf of our Lord the King government and administration of the kingdom'.

In May 1418 the people of Paris had risen against the Armagnacs, killed thousands of them – including their leader the Count of

FALAISE

Falaise was one of the last military strongholds to be surrendered at the end of the Hundred Years War. The English occupied it for more than 30 years.

The town's skyline today is still dominated by the splendid medieval castle, flying a bright red flag from the top of a traditional round tower standing above a massive square keep and turreted walls. It is all that a castle should be. Set on a rocky mound high above a little lake and the surrounding town, it forms a natural fortress.

The castle is the creation of alternating English and French construction. The main keep dates from the twelfth-century and was built by William the Conqueror's son, who was both King Henry I of England and Duke of Normandy. In the thirteenth-century the English King John (John Lackland) lost it – and a lot more territory besides – to his French rival Philip Augustus, who had the tower built. Then, when the castle fell to Henry V in the Hundred Years War, the English made further alterations.

Perhaps the most controversial 'improvements' were made in the 1990s by the modern French architect Bruno de Caris in an extensive renovation scheme. His grey concrete and steel façade, complete with drawbridge, in a sharply distinctive modern style, was the source of much local controversy. But during the self-guided tour of the interior, it is hard not to admire de Caris's bold heavy glass floors and bright canopy roofs.

The full history of the castle is still being pieced together and excavations continue. In the absence of definitive knowledge, a degree of patriotism has crept into the rival accounts of how the tower came to be called the Talbot Tower. Since it was built by Philip Augustus, the obvious explanation to the French is that there must have been a thirteenth-century Norman engineer called Talbot, so this is what the local tourist literature says. However, the resident English guide dismisses this as French propaganda and tells a different story. Because the castle was occupied by the English for so long during the Hundred Years War, and because the most famous English commander in France during the occupation was John Talbot, clearly the tower was named after him.

Falaise is also famous for two other historical reasons. It was the birthplace of William the Conqueror. You can visit the fountain at which in 1027 the beautiful Arlette, a tanner's daughter, was doing her washing with her skirts drawn up when she caught the eye of Robert, son of the then Duke of Normandy: William was to be their illegitimate child. Also, following the Allied landings in Normandy in 1944, Falaise gave its name to a major Second World War battlefield known as the Falaise Pocket or the Falaise Gap: a small 1944 museum in the town and another overlooking the actual battlefield give accounts of this.

The other site to visit is Mont Myrrha, the only other rocky mound in the town, adjacent to the mound supporting the castle. It offers a fine view, which is, of course, why attacking armies in the Middle Ages used to climb it and set up huge wooden catapults on top, in order to chuck large boulders a hundred yards across the intervening valley at the castle.

TROYES

As Queen Isabeau's temporary capital and the town in which Henry V was married, Troyes, in Champagne, played a significant role in the story of the Hundred Years War. It also of course gave its name to the Treaty of Troyes, which the French subsequently regarded with such shame.

In the Middle Ages it was a thriving commercial centre, across both the Flanders–Italy and the Paris–Germany trade routes, and it hosted the twice-yearly champagne fairs. The winter fair was held near the church of Saint Remy, where a nineteenth-century iron market hall houses the town market today. The summer fair was held near the church of Saint-Jean, in which Henry V and Catherine of France were married.

Although a major fire in 1524 necessitated much rebuilding in the sixteenth-century, Troyes still has much of the character of a medieval town. The areas around the cathedral and around the church of Saint-Jean have narrow streets and wooden-framed houses leaning at alarming angles. The rooftops on either side of the ruelle des Chats lean so closely towards one another that a cat can easily jump across the alley.

The place du Marché au Pain nearby, formerly the place aux Changes, was where the medieval moneychangers carried out their trade. The surrounding area, centred on the rue Champeaux, is attractively pedestrianized and crammed with cafés and restaurants. Without the cars it is now easier to feel you are in a medieval town.

Troyes has a rich collection of churches. The cathedral, which has fine stained-glass windows, was where Henry V, Queen Isabeau and the Duke of Burgundy signed the Treaty of Troyes. A plaque at the base of one of the towers commemorates Joan of Arc's liberation of the town from the English as she passed through here en route to Reims for the Dauphin's coronation.

The oldest church in Troyes is the twelfth-century Eglise Sainte-Madeleine, whose most striking feature today is a magnificent rood-screen added in the sixteenth-century. The thirteenth-century Basilique St-Urbain has a lively set of medieval gargoyles and, this being champagne country, a statue of the Virgin Mary holding Jesus in one hand and a bunch of grapes in another.

By the sixteenth-century the heyday of the champagne fairs had passed but Troyes flourished as a centre for hosiery and knitwear. Sixteenth-century buildings have been put to public use. The Hôtel de Mauroy now houses a museum of traditional hand tools. The Hôtel de Vaului-sant has both a museum recounting the history of Troyes and the Hosiery Museum.

Modern Troyes is known for its Magasins d'Usine (factory shops), in which companies such as Nike and Lacoste sell their wares direct to the consumer. The origin of this development was a decision by Petit Bâteau to sell to its employees slightly faulty goods, which could not otherwise be marketed. Now the commercial centre where this activity is based has become almost a modern trade fair, offering shoppers from far afield savings of 30–50 per cent on designer-label retail prices.

Over the centuries Troyes has maintained its reputation for trade and enterprise and done its best to live down its association with the infamous treaty of 1420.

Armagnac – and invited the Duke of Burgundy back into the capital. Charles VI welcomed him and thanked him for his kindness to the Queen! John the Fearless was now the principal source of power at the French court.

In 1415 the Dauphin Louis had died, followed in 1417 by his brother John, so the only other contender was the next brother in line for the throne, the new Dauphin Charles. He was an unprepossessing and politically inexperienced teenager, whose legitimacy – given Queen Isabeau's promiscuous sex life – was open to doubt. But Charles did not give way and instead, from a base south of the Loire at **Bourges** (featured in Chapter Six), declared himself a rival regent to his mother.

By 1419 John the Fearless was becoming apprehensive about Henry V's widening power base, and hence he agreed to meet the Dauphin Charles with the aim of resolving their differences. Charles, aged 16, had a different plan in mind. The meeting took place on 10 September on the bridge at Montereau, where the River Yonne meets the Seine, south-east of Paris. One of Charles's knights – it was said, on Charles's signal – attacked John the Fearless with a battle-axe and cleft his skull.

The naivety of this political murder, if it was a deliberate act, swiftly became apparent. John's son and heir as Duke of Burgundy, Philip (known to posterity as Philip the Good), swiftly formed an alliance with Henry V. If John the Fearless had been ambivalent about Henry V's growing power, Philip, in a mood of grief and revenge, promptly committed to helping Henry conquer France. The killing on the bridge at Montereau thus became one of the critical moments in the Hundred Years War. A century later a monk, displaying John the Fearless' damaged skull at the ducal mausoleum in Dijon, declared 'This is the hole through which the English entered France'.

On Christmas Day 1419 Henry V and Philip the Good, Duke of Burgundy signed their alliance. Henry was now determined on securing the throne of France for himself and his heirs, by marrying Princess Catherine and treating King Charles VI and Queen Isabeau as his in-laws. Henry's brother John, Duke of Bedford, would marry Philip's sister, Anne of Burgundy. Charles VI was persuaded to disinherit the Dauphin Charles, on the grounds that his complicity in the murder of John the Fearless made him unfit to be king. Queen Isabeau agreed, which helped lend credence to rumours that Charles was a bastard. She too publicly condemned the Dauphin's actions and approved those of Philip the Good.

Henry V's Triumph

In May 1420 Henry and Philip rode together into Troyes where the King, the Queen and Princess Catherine awaited them. The main elements of the Treaty of Troyes were now in place. To spare the dignity of Charles VI, and to avoid involving the Duke of Burgundy in deposing him, it was agreed that Charles should remain the nominal King of France for what seemed likely to be his last few remaining years, but that Henry should become regent, should marry the Princess Catherine and, on Charles's death, Henry and his heirs would inherit the crown. The treaty was signed on 21 May.

> Charles by the Grace of God, King of France. To all our Bailiffs, Provosts, Seneschals, and to all our chief officers of justice, greetings. Be it known that in sign of lasting agreement and perpetual peace we have, in this town of Troyes, just concluded and sworn a treaty between us and our most dear and well-beloved son Henry, King of England, heir and regent of France, in his name and our own on behalf of the crowns of France and England, in token of his marriage to our dearly-beloved daughter Catherine and of other articles made and agreed between us for the welfare and good of ourselves and our subjects and for the security of this country...
>
> ITEM it is agreed that immediately upon our decease and for all time thereafter the crown and sovereignty of France with all rights and appurtenances thereunto belonging shall be transferred in perpetuity to our said son Henry and his heirs.
>
> ITEM since we are for the most part prevented from attending to the cares and government of our kingdom, the practice and exercise of governing and ordering the public weal shall for the duration of our life be given over to our said son Henry, with the Council of Nobles and wise men who are in our obedience.

Henry was to keep Normandy, receive the 'homage' of Brittany and should also conquer the territory occupied by the 'pretended Dauphin'. Symbolically, Henry sealed the treaty with the seal that had been used at Brétigny in 1360. Twelve days later, still in Troyes, he and Catherine were married.

Two days after that Henry and Philip the Good rode out of Troyes together to continue the military campaign. First they took Sens, then Montereau, where John the Fearless's body was retrieved to be carried back to Dijon for burial. Next they laid siege to Melun, which was staunchly defended by Armagnac and Dauphinist supporters, aided by 20 Scots. The Anglo–Burgundian army of about 20,000 was probably the largest Henry led in France but it suffered from dysentery. Melun held out for four months. When it capitulated, Henry had the Scots hanged.

Then in December Henry made his ceremonial entry into Paris, riding side by side with Charles VI, and closely followed by Philip the Good of Burgundy and by Henry's two brothers, John, Duke of Bedford and Thomas, Duke of Clarence. The next day Queen Catherine arrived. Enguerrand de Monstrelet contrasts the two royal courts:

> At the season of Christmas the two kings and their queens held open court in the city of Paris, the King of France in his Hôtel de Saint-Pol, the King of England in the Louvre. But there was a vast difference between the state they kept, for the King of France was poorly served and attended by comparison with the great and mighty state he used to maintain, and on that day he received few visits apart from a small number of old servants and persons of low degree...
>
> As for the King and Queen of England, it is scarcely possible to tell in detail of the state they kept that day, of the feasts and ceremony and luxury of their court ... Subjects of the noble kingdom of France came from all parts in the greatest humility to do the king honour.

Finally, in January 1421, after more than three years' absence, Henry V returned with his French queen to England. He could reasonably have assumed that, within a few years, he would be crowned king of France.

CHAPTER SIX

The 'Goddams'

English Imperialism

Caesar famously observed that Gaul was divided into three parts. Henry V's military and diplomatic victories produced a similar division of France – into English, Burgundian and Dauphinist territory. Henry V, as Charles VI's regent, began to impose English rule over much of northern France, as well as retaining Aquitaine. His ally, Philip the Good, held his own territories as Duke of Burgundy. The Dauphin Charles sought to sustain a rival French regime with its power base in central and south-east France (see Map 12, p. 138).

In reality, the pattern of control was more complex, fluid and messy. The English-held territory did not form a single block. The long-standing English duchy of Aquitaine continued to be fairly self-contained, separated from the north by Dauphinist France. Henry V paid it relatively little attention.

The heart of the new English imperialism was Normandy, with its centre of government at **Rouen** (see feature). Because of the English connection going back to the time of William the Conqueror, Henry regarded Normandy rather differently from the rest of northern France and began a serious attempt to colonize and govern it. In the rest of northern France, which Henry expected to inherit from Charles VI, the English could only hope to maintain control in practice by relying heavily on their close alliance with the Burgundians. Even then, pockets of loyalty to the former Orléanist and Armagnac causes, for example around Vaucouleurs in Lorraine, bred hostility to the Anglo-Burgundian establishment.

ROUEN

Flaubert's *Madame Bovary* came to Rouen to escape the provincialism of small-town life. It is a metropolitan city. Perhaps the best introduction to it is the panoramic view from the Corniche off to the south-east, from which you see side by side the industrialized inland port along the left bank of the Seine and the gothic spires pointing up from the right bank. Rouen has a strong cultural and artistic tradition. It was the birthplace of Corneille, as well as of Flaubert, and Monet's paintings of the west front of Rouen Cathedral are among the best known works of French Impressionism.

Rouen was also England's capital in France under the fifteenth-century dual monarchy. The Duke of Bedford, who spent so much of his life here, is buried in its cathedral. However, the city's population fell sharply after Henry V's cruel siege of 1418 and, conscientious though Bedford was as regent, its economy suffered during the ensuing 30 years of English occupation. Rouen's wonderful flamboyant buildings, like the law courts, date from the period of prosperity that followed the expulsion of the 'Goddams'.

Shamingly, England's principal contribution to the history of Rouen was the burning of Joan of Arc. A plaque on the archbishop's palace shows where she was tried; the last surviving tower of Philip Augustus's castle here is where she was tortured; the elegant gothic church of Saint-Ouen is where she briefly recanted; and a 65 foot high cross stands beside the site of the pyre in the old market place where she was burned. Next to it is a modern market and a curvaceous modern church, built in 1979 but incorporating stained glass windows rescued from a sixteenth-century church destroyed in 1944. Leading to the church entrance is a long and elegant porch on whose wall is inscribed André Malraux's dedication 'JEANNE, SANS SEPULCHRE ET SANS PORTRAIT, TOI QUI SAVAIS QUE LE TOMBEAU DES HEROS EST LE COEUR DES VIVANTS'.

Half-timbered houses line the marketplace and extend along attractive pedestrianized cobbled streets to the cathedral and beyond. There is a fine walk along the rue du Gros Horloge, underneath the archway surmounted by Rouen's famously ornate clock. Continue down the rue Saint-Romain, alongside the cathedral and the booksellers' court. Then go up the rue Damiette into the rue Eau-de-Robec, which has a stream, crossed by footbridges, running down its middle. Nearby is the fifteenth-century church of Saint-Maclou and the extraordinary Aitre Saint-Maclou, a cloistered square, which served as a medieval cemetery and then as an ossuary, where macabre images of skulls and bones have been carved into the wooden pillars.

The cathedral is Rouen's gothic masterpiece. Assymetrical towers flank an elaborately decorated west front rich in carvings. The tall central lantern tower, made of cast iron, is flanked by four smaller spires (one of which was toppled through the cathedral roof by France's dramatic storm of 1999). The interior of the central tower heightens the nave. Around the ambulatory lie effigies of the first two dukes of Normandy, Rollo and William Longsword. In the Lady Chapel are the Renaissance tombs of the cardinals of Amboise and of the husband of Diane de Poitiers (she is portrayed weeping).

Rouen has a distinguished collection of paintings in its Fine Arts Museum. It also has museums devoted to pottery and to wrought ironwork, and a Musée Corneille, a Musée Flaubert and a Musée Jeanne d'Arc – whose display ends with an invitation to visit www.jeanne-darc.com.

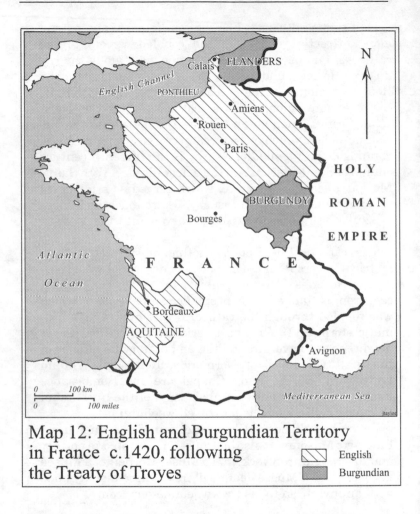

Map 12: English and Burgundian Territory
in France c.1420, following
the Treaty of Troyes

⧅ English
▨ Burgundian

The English occupation was not popular. The English were known as the 'Goddams' – corrupted into 'Godons' in French – no doubt because of their soldiers' constant use of this adjective. In the first few years English rule was harsh. After starving Rouen into submission, Henry V had imposed a punitive fine on its citizens, many of whom fled. The population of Harfleur had also been expelled to make way for colonists. In Normandy as a whole, local administrators were appointed and the French language remained in use, but positions of authority were given to Englishmen as an incentive to remain and settle. The English held the castles and dominated the region militarily. Increasingly, the French footed the bills. After a poor harvest in 1420, starvation was widespread and the population fell sharply. Henry V was a determined conqueror and an admired soldier, but he did little to win the affection of the new kingdom he expected to rule.

The Dauphin Charles had his centre of government south of the Loire at **Bourges** (see feature). His position was not strong. He had been disinherited by King Charles VI and Queen Isabeau and undermined by persistent rumours of his illegitimacy. The duchy of Brittany had chosen to ally itself to Charles VI and Henry V – at any rate for the present. And the powerful Duke of Burgundy, Philip the Good, remained his sworn enemy on account of the murder of his father at Montereau. Nonetheless, central and south-east France was unlikely to switch its loyalty to the Anglo-Burgundians so the Dauphin had a heartland from which he could draw troops and revenue. He also courted England's traditional Scottish foes and secured the services of an able Scottish military commander, the Earl of Buchan.

It was almost impossible to picture the Dauphin defeating the trio of Charles VI, Henry V and Philip the Good – but, equally, the King of England could not fully enforce his entitlement, by treaty, to be the next king of France unless the Dauphin capitulated.

Henry V's Last Campaign

When Henry V returned to England with his new French queen, he left his brother Thomas, Duke of Clarence, in charge of military operations against the Dauphin.

In 1421 Clarence and Thomas Montague, Earl of Salisbury (who was probably England's most outstanding general) conducted a raid south into the territory along the Loire without at first meeting much organized resistance. On Easter Saturday, separated temporarily both from Salisbury and from the formidable English archers, Clarence

BOURGES

Bourges prospered during the Middle Ages. In the thirteenth-century it built a richly decorated cathedral. In the
fourteenth-century John, Duke of Berry, a generous
patron of the arts, had his capital here. Then in the fifteenth-century, when the Dauphin Charles was forced to
flee here from the Anglo-Burgundian regime ensconced in
Paris, Bourges flourished afresh as the centre of his rival
royal court. While Charles also resided at places such as
Chinon, Loches, and Poitiers, which were closer to the
frontiers with the English, Bourges provided a safe centre
both for him and for his courtiers.

The most prominent courtier here, and arguably Bourges's most famous citizen ever, was the merchant and
financier, Jacques Coeur, who contributed much of the
funding that later underpinned Charles' ultimate victory
over the English. His 'palace', an amazingly rich bourgeois
town house, is one of Bourges's principal tourist attractions today.

Jacques Coeur was neither modest nor restrained in his
taste. Carved into the flamboyant facade, looking out of
simulated windows on either side of the gateway, are two
figures representing the master and mistress of the house.
Lively and amusing carved figures also decorate pillars,
arches and fireplaces around the house. Shields with shell
and heart motifs, Jacques Coeur's crest, are everywhere. A
stone carving and a stained-glass window portray ships,
celebrating Jacques Coeur's trading empire.

The house itself is a treat – with seven spiral staircases,
a splendid banqueting hall with a musicians'gallery, carvings depicting cooking over the doorway to the kitchens,
carvings of religious activity showing the way to the gaudy
chapel, and elegantly curved wooden vaulting over the
long galleries around the central courtyard. Sadly posterity has had rather more enjoyment from the house than
Jacques Coeur did himself. He was arrested for financial

malpractice in 1451 before the building work was fully finished.

Bourges Cathedral is both magnificent and unusual. Its two towers are of different heights (and dates). Its west front has five ornate doorways, rich in carvings, mirrored inside by the central nave and four side aisles. The double ambulatory continues the line of these aisles and contains a very fine set of stained-glass windows. In the nave you can see a fifteenth-century astronomical clock. There are no transepts. The crypt is deep and spacious. You have to pay to enter it but the ticket also covers a climb up the north tower for a view spanning the whole city and beyond.

While a major fire in 1487 did great damage, the narrow streets and half-timbered houses around the rue Mirebeau, the rue Coursalon and the place Gordaine evoke medieval Bourges. The carvings on the Maison de la Reine Blanche in the rue Gambon are particularly interesting. The Renaissance Hôtel Cujas, Hôtel Lallemant and Hôtel des Echévins all now house museums – the last mentioned being a gallery devoted to the work of the twentieth-century local artist, Maurice Estève.

Bourges is a jolly place. Bright banners hang over the main streets; the archbishop's formal garden now serves as a park with a café; the Prés-Fischaux Gardens form another attractive setting; the city water tower has been decorated; even the post office has an early Renaissance character (albeit from the 1920s). The Dauphin Charles was called 'the King of Bourges' as an insult – but one could do a lot worse in life.

learned of a Franco-Scots force nearby, at a place called Baugé, and set off with a small troop to fight it.

It was an impulsive act, based on inadequate intelligence. The Franco-Scots force proved to be more than three times as large as Clarence's troop. Clarence at first thought he had done well, only to discover that he was merely fighting the Franco-Scots vanguard. Their main army, under the Earl of Buchan, then appeared and slaughtered the English force. Clarence was among the dead subsequently retrieved by the Earl of Salisbury.

Though a small battle, Baugé was a calamity for Henry V. Clarence was both his brother and, at the time, his heir. In June 1421, Henry therefore returned to France, bringing additional troops and siege equipment, intent now on subduing the Dauphinist south.

Landing at Calais, he first had to consolidate the Anglo-Burgundian hold on Picardy. Then he marched south and relieved the Dauphinist siege of Chartres. After capturing some nearby towns along the Loire, he turned north-east to attack Meaux, whose garrison had been raiding Paris from the east.

Henry V began the siege of Meaux in early October 1421. The town was protected by what was almost a huge moat. It lay in a bend of the River Marne and on the side away from the river a canal had been constructed. Following heavy autumn rains the whole area became flooded and water-logged. The English siege engines and cannon achieved little. Henry was still encamped in front of Meaux on 6 December when, back in England, Queen Catherine gave birth to their son, and his heir, who was also christened Henry.

Disease had spread in the damp English camp and Henry himself fell ill, probably from dysentery. He stayed with his army and a physician came across from England. The townspeople of Meaux, by now starving, surrendered in March 1422 but the garrison held out against the English artillery until May. By then Henry was seriously ill. He continued to try and lead his army during June and July but he had difficulty riding and needed to be carried on a litter. After rallying briefly, he relapsed. It became clear that he was dying. In August 1422 he was carried back to Vincennes, near Paris, and it was here, with members of his family at his bedside, that he spent the last three weeks of his life.

Henry had two surviving brothers with a potential interest in his political legacy – John, Duke of Bedford, the elder of the two, whom he trusted, and Humphrey, Duke of Gloucester, who was more volatile. It was to Bedford that Henry bequeathed his responsibilities in France. The chronicler Enguerrand de Monstrelet records Henry as saying:

> Dear brother John, I beseech you on the loyalty and love you have always shown me, to show the same loyalty and consideration to my fair son Henry your nephew. And I further charge you that, whatever errors you may make, you do not so long as you live suffer any treaty to be made with our enemy Charles de Valois, and in no circumstances allow the duchy of Normandy to be restored to him. If our fair brother of Burgundy should wish to undertake the regency of this realm of France, I advise you to grant it to him, but if he refuses it then take it on yourself.

Henry knew well the critical role of the alliance with Philip the Good, Duke of Burgundy, in sustaining the English position in France: 'I further entreat you as earnestly as I know how that you should not for any reason enter into disagreement with our fair brother of Burgundy – and this you must expressly recommend to our brother Humphrey – for if there were any ill will between you (which God forbid) the affairs of this realm, which are at present in a very healthy state, would soon worsen.'

On 31 August 1422 Henry V, King of England and heir to the King of France, died at Vincennes, aged 35. His coffin was taken first to **Saint-Denis** (see feature in Chapter Four), the traditional burial ground of the French monarchs, and then through Normandy, where the queen joined the procession, to Calais and back to England. The death sent out shock waves of grief mixed with apprehension. Henry V had reigned for only nine and a half years. A great warrior, cut down by disease in his prime, he left a child heir not quite nine months old. Less than two months later, on 22 October, King Charles VI of France died.

The Dual Monarchy

So instead of Henry V becoming king of both England and France, achieving at last the title Edward III had claimed at Ghent back in 1340, that honour fell to his baby son. One king would rule both realms – Henry VI of England who, at any rate in the eyes of those who lived north of the Loire, was also 'Henri II' of France.

In practical terms, as Henry V had wished, English rule in France was in the hands of John, Duke of Bedford. Pledged to marry Philip the Good's sister, Anne of Burgundy, Bedford needed no persuasion of the importance of the Burgundian alliance and, as his dying brother had advised, gave Philip first refusal of the position of regent in France before taking on the role himself.

In England Humphrey, Duke of Gloucester was conspicuously not given the position of regent. Rather he was styled Protector and, while he had charge of the realm, he had to cede precedence whenever Bedford returned to England.

Bedford was committed and conscientious in his role as Regent of France. He liked the country and administered it benignly, while endeavouring to consolidate the Anglo-Burgundian regime militarily. Over the period 1423–24 he made substantial progress. An alliance between England, Burgundy and Brittany isolated the Dauphin who was dismissed contemptuously as 'the King of Bourges'. Anglo-Burgundian forces made raids on the Dauphinists in several areas and, at Cravant in 1423, the Earl of Salisbury halted a Dauphinist (and Scots) attack on Burgundy.

The decisive battle of this period was fought at Verneuil, on the southern border of Normandy, in 1424. Bedford was clearing Normandy of any residual Dauphinist support prior to making a concerted attack on the Dauphin's territory along the Loire. Under his field commanders, the Earl of Salisbury and John Talbot, later Earl of Shrewsbury, he had an army of about 10,000. Learning that a small Scots force, allied to the Dauphin, had just tricked their way into occupying the town of Verneuil, Bedford set off to recapture it. Meanwhile, the Dauphin had assembled a much bigger army, probably more than 15,000 strong, including about 6,000 Scots mercenaries and some Italian cavalry. Remaining south of the Loire himself, he despatched this army, commanded by the Count of Aumale, the Earl of Buchan and the Earl of Douglas, to confront and forestall Bedford's advance.

A pitched battle took place in front of the town of Verneuil. Bedford deployed his archers and men-at-arms on foot in much the same fashion as at Poitiers and Agincourt but, in addition, kept a reserve of archers in the rear guarding the English baggage and horses. The Dauphinists too formed into traditional blocks, awaiting attack, keeping their cavalry on the flanks. The English advanced and engaged the Dauphinists in heavy hand-to-hand combat. By the account of the chronicler Jean de Wavrin, 'the blood of the dead spread on the field and that of the wounded ran in great streams all over the earth.'

Critically, Dauphinist cavalry attacks around the English flanks were halted and repelled by the English archers in reserve, who then counterattacked. The Dauphinist forces faltered and the English regrouped for a further attack. The French began to flee while the Scots who held the field were massacred. The Count of Aumale, the Earl of Buchan and the Earl of Douglas were all killed. Among the prisoners was the Duke of Alençon, whose ransom was to earn his captor, Sir John Fastolf, £13,000. In total the Dauphinist casualties numbered about 7,000 and, as Bedford noted later, 'The moste vengeance fell upon the proud Scottes.'

Bedford had achieved a considerable strategic advantage by destroying the only major Dauphinist army, but that same year, 1424, he was struggling to hold together the English alliance with Philip of Burgundy. The source of his difficulty was his brother Humphrey, Duke of Gloucester.

The previous year Humphrey had married the beautiful Jacqueline, Countess of Hainault, a woman with a history. Jacqueline had inherited in her own right the county of Hainault in the Low Countries, which was adjacent to the Duke of Burgundy's territories and on which Duke Philip the Good had designs. After being widowed at an early age, Jacqueline had been married to Philip's ally, John of Brabant. But she hated the marriage and in 1421 deserted her husband and fled to England. There she met Humphrey, Duke of Gloucester, and, having obtained a somewhat dubious papal agreement to the annulment of her previous marriage, took him as her third husband. She then made Humphrey heir to Hainault and urged him to invade the Low Countries and take it by force from John of Brabant. So, in the autumn of 1424, Humphrey landed in Calais with a small force and occupied Hainault. Philip the Good arrived with a bigger army; Jacqueline was captured; and Humphrey fled. A new Pope declared that Jacqueline and Humphrey's marriage had been invalid and, in any event, Humphrey took up with one of Jacqueline's ladies-in-waiting.

While the whole episode was farcical, its political effect was significant. In France the Duke of Bedford, the Regent, was married to Philip the Good's sister and was supposedly his staunch ally – an alliance on which English policy in relation to France was founded. Yet Bedford's brother, the Duke of Gloucester, Protector of England, led an invasion force into the Low Countries against Philip the Good's army. Later that autumn an angry Philip the Good told Bedford that he was reconsidering the Anglo-Burgundian alliance against the Dauphin. Bedford's wife, Anne, did her best to keep her husband and her brother on good terms.

Despite these difficulties, Bedford managed to maintain the credibility of the dual monarchy in Anglo-Burgundian France. In 1427 after a period of wrestling with affairs back in England, he was able to consolidate good relations with Philip the Good and win back the wavering allegiance of the Duke of Brittany. For Normandy the clear-cut victory at Verneuil had brought a lull in the constant warfare and a period of relative tranquillity. Bedford could not make English rule popular, nor eliminate the looting and robbery perpetrated either by English garrisons or by English deserters and highwaymen. He had no qualms about taxing the locals or about rewarding English 'settlers'. However, he also rewarded the local French even if they were unlikely ever to reach the highest positions of authority. He established links with the Church and with the University of Paris. He founded a new university at Caen. Touchingly, he called his own house in Rouen '*Joyeux Repos*'.

In 1428 Bedford felt ready for a further assault on the Dauphin and assembled fresh troops for an expedition that the Earl of Salisbury would lead along the Loire. He and Salisbury debated whether to invade Anjou, and thus join up English rule in Normandy with English rule in Aquitaine, or, alternatively, to attack **Orléans** (see feature, p. 150–1), striking more directly at the Dauphin's power base.

Strictly speaking, an English attack on Orléans would breach the rules of chivalry since its lord, the Duke of Orléans, had been a prisoner in England ever since Agincourt. However, the city was defended by the Duke's half-brother, Dunois, known as the Bastard of Orléans. So, putting their scruples aside, Bedford and Salisbury agreed that Orléans should be their target.

First, Salisbury took the surrounding towns of Jargeau, Beaugency and Meung (see Map 13, p. 148). Then, having cut off its supply routes, and with an offer of help from a Burgundian force, he laid siege to Orléans. The first main English assault was on the two tower for-tification, known as 'Les Tourelles', on the southern end of the bridge across the Loire into the city (see Map 14, p. 149). Towards the end of October 1428, Salisbury captured and occupied this stronghold. Destroying an arch in the bridge behind them, the Dauphinist defen-ders retreated into the fortified city on the north bank – where Salis-bury confidently expected them to starve.

The Siege of Orléans

The English capture of the Tourelles, however, was followed by a sudden accident. The next day Salisbury was inspecting the French position from an upper floor in the Tourelles when he was hit in the face by an iron bar dislodged from a window by a gunstone, probably unleashed by a French schoolboy. Eight days later he died from this wound. Command passed to the less gifted Earl of Suffolk who mis-takenly gave Dunois an opportunity to strengthen the defending Dauphinist garrison.

The siege continued into 1429, with Talbot taking charge of the English army. Their morale was boosted when Sir John Fastolf, com-manding a troop escorting 300 wagons of foodstuffs, including salted herrings, to feed the English besiegers, intercepted and defeated a Dauphinist-Scottish relief force. This encounter went down in history as 'the Battle of the Herrings'.

However, the Dauphinists then secured a further advantage by diplomacy. They sent an embassy to the Duke of Burgundy, Philip the Good, and proposed that, as the rightful Duke of Orléans was still a

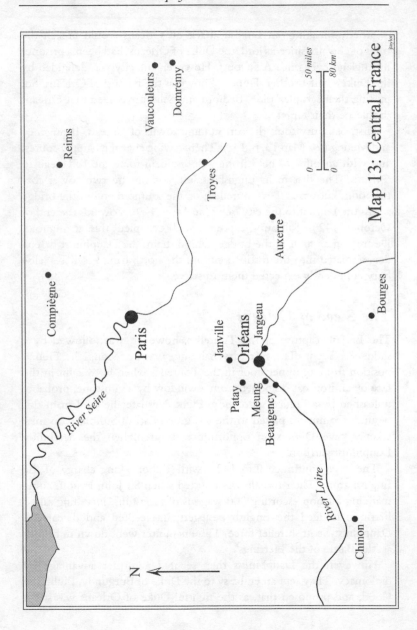

Map 13: Central France

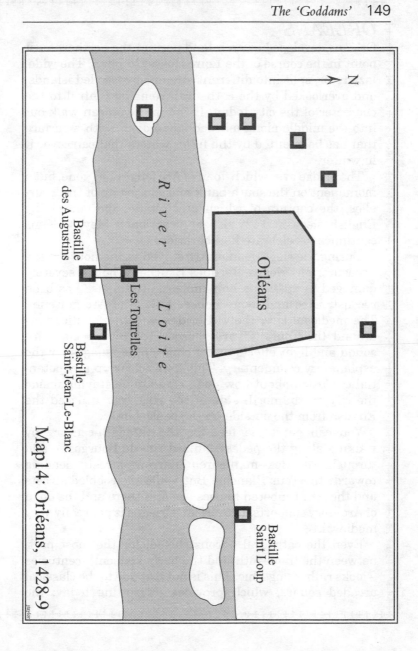

Map 14: Orléans, 1428-9

ORLEANS

Orléans developed as an inland port, at the northernmost point in the course of the Loire closest to Paris. The wide, lazy river, split into different streams by wooded islands, and overlooked by the cathedral, remains central to the character of the city today. In summer you can walk out into the middle along a broad stone dyke, with a surface that has been pitted by the fuller waters that can cover it in winter.

The bridge over which Joan of Arc fought has gone, but a monument on the south bank marks the site of the Tourelles, the capture of which precipitated the end of the English siege in 1429. Every year, on 8 May, Orléans continues to celebrate its liberation.

During the siege Joan of Arc stayed in the house of the Treasurer of Orléans, Jacques Boucher. Though severely damaged in 1940, his half-timbered red house has been reconstructed and today houses a Joan of Arc museum. The medieval city, the old bridge and the fortifications around the Tourelles are represented by models, with sound and light effects and a choice of languages for the explanatory commentary. This helps clear up any potential confusion about how Joan came to be staying inside the city on the north side of the river yet attacked the English from the outside on the south bank.

You can get some feel for the fifteenth-century by walking along the pedestrianized rue de Bourgogne and through the less-manicured narrow streets leading towards the Tour Blanche. But while the cobbled streets and the half-timbered houses are still there and the Joan of Arc story supports its tourism, Orléans is not really very medieval.

Even the cathedral – constructed, for the most part, between the thirteenth and the early sixteenth-centuries – looks rather ungothic. This is not just due to the classical arcaded square, which provides its setting today: the cathedral itself, damaged in the Wars of Religion, was restored with seventeenth and eighteenth-century reinterpretations of gothic, most obviously in the lantern towers above the west facade and the statues around the doorways below. Inside the cathedral, the tombs of three Scots who died fighting on the French side provide a reminder of the Hundred Years War, but the finest features are the early eighteenth-century wooden carvings around the choir.

A short distance north of the cathedral is the red-brick Renaissance Hôtel Groslot, where various French kings stayed when passing through the city. Inside the courtyard, in front of the main staircase, is a nineteenth-century statue of Joan of Arc by the Princess Marie of Orléans, donated by her father, the Orléanist king, Louis Philippe. The gardens behind the Hôtel Groslot now house the ruined facade of the fifteenth-century Chapel of Saint-Jacques. Another Renaissance hotel houses a display of the life and works of the writer Charles Péguy, who was killed in battle in 1914.

The splendidly elegant arcades of the eighteenth-century rue Royale lead in one direction down to the Pont Royal (now named after George V), which replaced the medieval bridge across the Loire. At the other end lies the place du Martroi, to whose open-air cafés and restaurants eight other streets and boulevards (not to mention the modern bronze-coloured trams) also conspire to lead you. In the centre, of course, is an equestrian statue of Joan of Arc.

prisoner in England, the city should for the present be ceded to Philip as his cousin. The English should be required to withdraw, but would be paid some revenue, and Philip should govern Orléans.

While this proposal was tantamount to a face-saving Dauphinist surrender, it had the effect, no doubt intended, of producing a split in the Anglo–Burgundian alliance. Philip the Good favoured the idea. Bedford wanted Orléans for the dual monarchy, not for Burgundy, and declared that he would be 'very angry to have beaten the bushes that others might take the birds'. Philip the Good was then angry in turn and withdrew his Burgundian troops from the siege, seriously depleting the force Talbot and his colleagues could deploy. Such was the position at the end of April 1429 when a young farm girl of about 19, dressed in male clothing, made her dramatic entry into Orléans.

Joan of Arc had grown up in **Domrémy** (see feature, p. 154–5), near Vaucouleurs in Lorraine in north-east France. Illiterate, deeply pious, chaste, and unwilling to marry the suitor favoured by her parents, Joan had left home and come to the warfront on the Loire with a mission. She had heard 'voices', which she ascribed to Saint Michael, Saint Catherine and Saint Margaret, urging her to relieve the siege of Orléans and lead the Dauphin to his coronation.

Why her religious experiences should have had so precise a military and political focus is a matter of conjecture. Vaucouleurs, under its local nobleman Robert de Baudricourt, was a Dauphinist island in Burgundian north-east France. In 1425 an Anglo–Burgundian band drove off the cattle and burned the church at Domrémy, while in 1428 a further attack caused the villagers to flee to the nearby town of Neufchâteau. The documentation from her subsequent trial records: 'Asked if the people of Domrémy sided with the Burgundians or the other party, she answered that she only knew one Burgundian; and she would have been quite willing for him to have his head cut off, that is if it had pleased God ... Asked if the voice told her in her youth to hate the Burgundians, she answered that since she had known that the voices were for the king of France, she did not like the Burgundians.'

De Baudricourt took some persuading but he finally agreed to send Joan, with an escort, across France to **Chinon** (see feature, p. 156–7) to see the Dauphin Charles and his court. Charles had her interrogated by a group of clerics, to check her religious beliefs, and inspected by his mother-in-law, Yolanda of Aragon, Queen of Sicily, to check her virginity. Satisfied on both scores, he gave her his trust.

Joan had a quality which Charles lacked: she had certainty. Charles did not know how to end the divisions of the country; he did not know if he could ever win militarily; he did not know whether he had been fathered by Charles VI; he did not know whether he would ever be crowned Charles VII – and, being uncertain, he did not inspire certainty in others. Joan did know, inwardly. Joan thought in terms of good and bad, right and wrong, without being troubled by any of the complexities, risks and doubts that breed uncertainty. As a chaste and religious girl, she was the ideal symbol of 'good' and 'right'. Joan did have the capacity to inspire – and Charles must have seen that her inspiration might work, provided the setting in which she was used did not require subtlety.

The Maid of Orléans

With the Burgundians gone, the siege of Orléans was now a less subtle matter: either the English would take it or the Dauphinists would expel them. Joan had a simple goal – which she magnified to driving the English out of France altogether. She sent them this letter:

JHESUS MARIA
King of England, and you, Duke of Bedford, who call yourself regent of the kingdom of France; you, William de la Pole, Earl of Suffolk; John, Lord Talbot, and you Thomas, Lord Scales, who call yourselves lieutenants of the said Duke of Bedford, acknowledge the summons of the King of Heaven, and render up to the Maid who is here sent by God, the King of Heaven, the keys of all the good towns you have here taken and violated in France. She is come here by God's will to reclaim the blood royal. She is very ready to make peace, if you will acknowledge her to be right by leaving France and paying for what you have held. And you, archers, companions of war, men-at-arms and others who are before the town of Orléans, go away into your own country, by God; and, if you do not do so, expect news of the Maid who will come to see you shortly, to your very great injury. King of England, if you do not do so I am chief-of-war, and in whatever place I

DOMREMY

Domrémy-la-Pucelle, in the valley of the River Meuse at the north end of the Vosges, is a village of one street. It's true that there are a few other roads but they have names such as the rue de Derrière le Village and the rue de Derrière l'Eglise. Standing on the bridge watching the cows wading in the river and looking at the wide-roofed farm buildings whose arched gateways line the one street, it is easy to picture the rural community in which Joan of Arc grew up.

You might have expected her birthplace to have become commercially colonized – perhaps with sentimental purple pictures and a Holiday Inn. But there are two reassuringly amateur souvenir shops, one calling itself a free museum, the other more of a general store, while the Hôtel Jeanne d'Arc is pleasantly surprised when anyone decides to stay there.

The Maison Natale was modified at the end of the fifteenth-century and a statue of Joan was later built over the doorway, but essentially it remains a simple four-roomed cottage. Next door is the church where Joan was baptised. While the interior has been reorganized, with the chancel now at the west end, you can still see the statue of Saint Margaret before which Joan prayed.

Behind the Maison Natale, in two discreetly designed modern buildings, is Le Centre Johannique, comprising archives and a visitor centre. It has a short storybook video about Joan's life pitched at family groups, a longer 'audio-visuel expérience' for the more arty, and a gallery of displays about medieval history to provide a deeper context.

The highlight of the gallery visit is a pageant, in which a group of life-size models of historical characters light up in turn as actors' voices conduct an orchestrated series of conversations encapsulating the plot of the Hundred Years War. Easy to mock, this pageant is actually rather impressive. It does not shy away from the full complexity of its subject. Not only are all the obvious characters represented, but a Turk describes the crusade in which John the Fearless fought – and Eleanor of Aquitaine pipes up from beneath her tombstone to explain how the whole saga of disputed sovereignty started by her switching royal husbands three centuries earlier. The conflict between the Burgundians and the Armagnacs is also described. Thus Joan of Arc is portrayed in the context of a French civil war and not simply as a patriotic resistance fighter against the wicked English invaders.

A couple of miles away, up on the hillside where Joan heard her 'voices', is a rather more extravagant memorial – the Basilica du Bois-Chenu. This dates from the late nineteenth and early twentieth-centuries, the period during which Joan was first declared venerable, then beatified, and finally canonized. While the setting is magnificent, the building may not suit all tastes. The tower starts with a layer of decorated arches, then a frieze, a balcony, arched stained-glass windows, another frieze, a pediment, more arches, more windows, more arches, the start of the spire roof, a set of angels supporting a crown, then the rest of the roof with a cross on the top. Then there is the dome, the porticos and a stairway of honour leading into a painted nave in which six large frescoes tell the story of Joan's life. It is floodlit at night.

CHINON

What distinguishes the château of Chinon from its fellow Loire châteaux is that it is largely ruined. This is not just a matter of age: the Richelieu family acquired it in the seventeenth-century and allowed it to deteriorate so that it did not outshine their own local abode. There they failed; it is the ruins of Chinon that draw the visitors today.

Stretched along an escarpment above the River Vienne, the château seems almost to sit on top of the town below it. Certainly, when you are in the old town, that is how it feels.

It was here that Joan of Arc came in 1429, after her ride across France, seeking an interview with the Dauphin Charles. So in the town today, you can see the area around the Grand Carroi where she probably stayed, the churches in which she probably prayed, and the square in which she may have practised military drill (now called the place Jeanne d'Arc and featuring a statue of Joan astride a very excited-looking horse).

Chinon does have some older history. The Fort Saint-George at the eastern end of the château, now almost completely ruined, was built by King Henry II of England. He and Eleanor of Aquitaine apparently regarded Chinon as their favourite residence. It is also said that Richard Coeur-de-Lion died in Chinon in 1199 after being mortally wounded at Chalus, further south. Chinon was then captured from Richard's brother, King John, by King Philip Augustus of France, who extended and strengthened its fortifications.

Visitors go into the château now over a drawbridge leading to the fourteenth-century Tour d'Horloge, which stands in good repair, four storeys high, and houses a Joan of Arc museum. Around an attractive grassy courtyard beyond are a number of ruined towers and ramparts, which you can explore.

On the south side is the set of Royal Apartments where the guides tell the full Joan of Arc story – aided by royal family trees, an audio-visual display, and a tableau of waxwork figures portraying the famous scene in which Joan meets the Dauphin for the first time and unerringly identifies him although he has hidden in disguise among his courtiers. Your guide may speculate heretically about whether she could have had an accomplice in the room. The Grande Salle in which this meeting actually took place is now in ruins but has a plaque to commemorate the event.

On the château visit, you are also told the story of how the Dauphin Charles used to visit his mistress, Agnès Sorel, by going through an underground passage leading from the château to her house nearby.

Chinon's other famous historical figure is Rabelais. You can visit his house and the caves in the cliff where he and his contemporaries used to store and drink their wine. Chinon has a museum devoted to the history of river traders on the Loire. There are several distinguished old houses, most notably the fourteenth-century Maison Rouge. On special weekends in August Chinon also mounts a colourful medieval market.

reach your people in France, I will make them quit it, willy-nilly. And if they will not obey, I will have them all slain; I am sent here by God, the King of Heaven, to drive you, body for body, out of the whole of France.'

So the Dauphin put the Duke d'Alençon in charge of organizing a new relief force for Orléans and, when it was assembled, put Joan, dressed in armour and carrying her standard, at its head. Dunois arranged a skirmish to divert the English, came out of Orléans to meet the relief force, and conducted it to a vantage point upriver from which the vital supplies could be ferried by barge down into the city. After dark he and Joan rode into Orléans at the head of their troop of soldiers and were greeted with great excitement. Joan had managed to get herself into Orléans; her next challenge was to get the English out. She was not militarily in charge of the Dauphinist forces within Orléans, but she seized the initiative and placed herself at their head.

Exhorted and inspired by her, the Dauphinists made three assaults on the English troops entrenched in the various *bastilles* that surrounded Orléans (see Map 14, p. 149). The first was on the Bastille Saint-Loup, on the north bank of the Loire, upriver to the east of the city. The Dauphinist attackers overthrew the English garrison there, making it easier, thereafter, for relief supplies to enter Orléans. The second attack, a couple of days later, involved crossing to the south bank of the Loire and attacking the Bastille Saint-Jean-le-Blanc. The English had only a small force there, which they withdrew into the Bastille des Augustins and then fought back vigorously. Urged on by Joan, the Dauphinists took this stronghold too and consolidated their position on the south bank.

The English now concentrated their defence on the Tourelles, at the south end of the broken bridge across the Loire. Here the Dauphinists made their third assault, firing artillery across the bridge from the north bank and harassing the English defenders by boat from the river, as well as launching their main infantry attack, with Joan at its head, from their new base on the south bank.

During one of many assaults by scaling ladder on the earthworks protecting the Tourelles on the south side, Joan was wounded in the neck by a crossbow bolt but, with the wound dressed, she returned to lead the fight again from the front. In the face of fierce English resistance, the Dauphinists finally manoeuvred a boat into position underneath the bridge adjoining the Tourelles and set it on fire. Amid the flames English resistance collapsed: the Dauphinists recaptured the Tourelles. The following day, 8 May, Talbot withdrew the English army. Joan had broken the siege of Orléans.

During the course of June 1429, a large Dauphinist army, led by the Duke of Alençon accompanied by Joan, recaptured the strategic Loire towns of Jargeau, Beaugency and Meung. At Jargeau the Earl of Suffolk was captured, having knighted his French captor to make sure he did not have to surrender to an opponent of low rank. But not much chivalry remained in the Dauphinists' relationship with the 'Goddams'. Most of the English prisoners taken at Jargeau were massacred.

Talbot had withdrawn the English army north of the Loire to Janville where he was joined by Sir John Fastolf. The latter advised withdrawing further north. Talbot overruled him and they set off back towards the Loire – until they learned the full size of the newly reinforced Dauphinist army, whereupon they began to retreat north again.

Alençon, with several other distinguished commanders as well as Joan and a force of more than 6,000 troops, caught the English rearguard, under Sir John Fastolf, near the town of Patay (see Map 13, p. 148). Fastolf tried to rally his scattering troops and to make contact with the vanguard, but the English army failed to deploy properly for battle and was overwhelmed.

It was a humiliating defeat. Some 2,000 English soldiers were killed at Patay. Talbot was captured. Fastolf, who escaped, was temporarily disgraced and deprived of his Garter – though this was later recognized to be an unjust verdict on his conduct.

Meanwhile the victorious Dauphinists, according to the chronicler Enguerrand de Monstrelet, 'returned to Orléans with all their prisoners and the booty they had taken from the English dead. They were welcomed with open arms by the people of that town, and special acclaim was given to Joan the Maid, because of whom, it seemed, their enemies had lost their will to resist and King Charles would be restored to his kingdom.'

King Charles VII

In the aftermath of these victories Joan was able to persuade the
Dauphin and his entourage to the next step in her vision. This was the
coronation of Charles in the traditional setting of the cathedral in
Reims (see feature, p. 162–3).

With an army of about 12,000 the Dauphinists set off across Anglo–
Burgundian territory to this cathedral city north-east of Paris of whose
allegiance they were uncertain (see Map 13, p. 148). It was a bold
course but, in the event, proved relatively uneventful. Auxerre offered
the Dauphinists money not to sack their town; **Troyes** surrendered
when threatened with a siege (see feature in Chapter Five). Reims,
whose archbishop accompanied the Dauphinist army, decided to open
its gates in welcome. As the Dauphin rode in, the Anglo–Burgundians
rode quietly out.

So, on 17 July 1429, in Reims cathedral the Dauphin was crowned
King Charles VII. The Archbishop of Reims presided over the ceremony. Charles was anointed with the holy oil used to consecrate the
kings of France, 'And, at the hour when the king was anointed, and also
when the crown was put on his head, everyone cried 'Noel!' and
trumpets sounded in such a manner, that it seemed that the vaults of the
church would split.'

No longer was Charles the Dauphin, to Joan or to his other followers. Joan knelt down before him, in tears, and said: 'Gentle king,
now the will of God has been accomplished, who wished that I should
raise the siege of Orléans and bring you to this city of Reims to receive
your solemn consecration, showing that you are the true king, that you
are he to whom the kingdom of France should belong.'

Joan, never a subtle strategist, was now for continuing the war.
Charles VII and some of his more wily courtiers, noting that Philip the
Good had conspicuously not done anything to impede the coronation,
were more interested in weaning Burgundy away from its English
alliance. The Duke of Burgundy had taken over from the English
responsibility for governing Paris. In the hope of winning over the
French capital without a fight, Charles VII now persuaded the Duke to
declare a 15-day truce. Joan had other ideas, as a letter she now wrote to

the citizens of Reims made clear: 'It is true that the King has made a fifteen day truce with the Duke of Burgundy by which he should render him the city of Paris peacefully at the end of the fortnight. However do not be surprised if I do not enter it as quickly; for a truce made in this way is so little to my liking, that I do not know if I shall keep it; but, if I keep it, it will only be to safeguard the honour of the king.'

Philip the Good did not, of course, surrender Paris. Joan led an assault on it, near the Porte Saint-Denis. She failed to win the day, and was wounded, but wished to try again. Bedford too was keen to provoke a battle. He sent Charles a letter mocking him for consorting with 'a disorderly and disgraced woman wearing the dress of a man.'

King Charles, however, concluded that head-on fighting was not the way to victory. He made a longer truce with the Duke of Burgundy, retreated south of the Loire once more, and disbanded his army. Joan was entrusted with some minor local military tasks, which she found frustrating.

The following year, 1430, Charles VII did not raise another army. He was now much less interested in warfare than in diplomacy. For Joan, the Burgundians remained the enemy but, for Charles, they were the potential ally that would enable the French to throw out the English for good.

When Philip the Good ordered his Burgundian captain, Jean de Luxembourg, to capture the town of Compiègne, north of Paris, Joan rushed to the aid of the local garrison. Ten days later, Joan rashly left the town to take part in a skirmish on its outskirts. According to the account of Enguerrand de Monstrelet,

> When the fighting had been going on for some time the French saw their enemies increasing in number and withdrew towards Compiègne, leaving the Maid with the rearguard and doing her best to encourage her men and bring them back without loss. But the Burgundians, knowing that help was quickly available on all sides, made a sudden attack on the French rear, at the conclusion of which (as I have been informed) the Maid was dragged from her horse by an archer... The French went back to Compiègne, wretched and angry at their defeat and particularly at the loss of the Maid. The Burgundians and the English, however, were more excited than if they had

REIMS

The most important date in Reims's history is either 498 or 499 (historians are not sure which). This was when Clovis, King of the Franks, was converted to Christianity and baptised here by the local bishop, Remy, linking Reims closely to both the medieval French monarchy and the church. From the ninth-century onwards the kings of France were anointed and crowned at Reims Cathedral, while the tomb of Bishop Remy became the foundation for the Basilica of Saint Remy in a nearby suburb. The cathedral and the basilica are still Reims's principal attractions today.

The towers of the gothic cathedral are immediately visible as you drive into Reims and the rue Libergier offers a long clear view of the west front – at its best, of course, in the late afternoon sun. On your left as you approach the cathedral is an equestrian statue of Joan of Arc, recalling the most famous royal coronation here, that of Charles VII.

The present cathedral building was constructed mainly between the thirteenth and fifteenth-centuries. Around the exterior are 2,300 sculptures. The west front hosts many of them but the three doorways of the north transept are also rich in detail. The simply decorated one on the right is from an earlier romanesque building. The elaborate central portal features both Saint Remy and Clovis, and the left-hand doorway has some lively corpses emerging from their tombs on Judgment Day either to join the elect in a cloth draped across Abraham's lap or to be added to the pot of the damned.

Around the top of the cathedral, just below the towers, are the tall and imposing statues of the Kings' Gallery. The central figure is Clovis and some 60 monarchs stand in niches stretching around the cathedral on either side of him. If you go on the tour of the cathedral – up the south-west tower and out onto the balcony – you encounter some of these stone giants. You can also walk on a platform above the stone ceiling of the nave in the 'attic' space below the wooden arched roof, see the clock, and go out around the guttering at the east end, looking down along the rows of flying buttresses.

Inside the cathedral, unusually, the internal wall of the west front is decorated with statuary. The chapel at the east end has a modern stained-glass window by Marc Chagall, picturing both Clovis's baptism and Charles VII with Joan of Arc.

Next door is the Palace of Tau, the archbishop's palace. It displays various relics, ornaments, copes, paintings and tapestries – and yet more cathedral statues.

If you then visit the Basilica of Saint Remy, it's a surprise to find so close another gothic edifice on such a large scale. Earlier and less ornate in style, and impressively high, it houses the tomb of Saint Remy, which was rebuilt in the nineteenth-century. The museum nearby includes a set of sixteenth-century tapestries depicting the saint's life.

Reims has plenty more to offer the visitor, from the Roman remains in the place du Forum to the eighteenth-century arcades of the place Royale. When you have had enough history, a visit to one of the champagne cellars for both an explanation and a tasting, or a drink and a meal in one of the brasseries along the place Drouet d'Erlon, will provide a refreshing contrast.

captured five hundred fighting men, for they had never been so much afraid of any captain or commander in war as they had been of the Maid.

Joan was handed over to Jean de Luxembourg who sold her to the English and their tame Burgundian cleric, Pierre Cauchon, Bishop of Beauvais (in whose diocese she had been captured). King Charles VII did not intervene – militarily, through negotiation, or even with legal arguments over the legitimacy of Cauchon's jurisdiction.

England's Revenge

That same spring, in 1430, just before Joan was captured, Bedford had brought the boy king Henry VI to France for the first time. They resided in Rouen for much of the following year and it was to Rouen that Joan was brought for trial. Joan had little doubt what the outcome would be. She told Jean de Luxembourg: 'I know well that the English will put me to death, believing after my death to gain the kingdom of France. But, were there a hundred thousand more "godons" than there are at present, they would not have the kingdom.'

Bedford almost certainly did want to see Joan condemned to death – and to be able to attribute Charles VII's recent successes to witchcraft – but, while he could influence Joan's trial, he was not in charge of it. This was to be an ecclesiastical process, involving the Inquisition, the University of Paris, and other learned theologians. Joan was asked whether Saint Margaret spoke to her in French, to which she replied 'Why should she speak English? She is not on the English side.' However, in general the substance of the trial was more religious than political and her accusers were French, albeit loyal to the Anglo-Burgundian regime.

The central charge was heresy. Joan was cross-examined about hearing saints' voices, her claim to know the will of God and whether she would obey the Church if her 'voices' gave her a different command. She was also questioned about her letter to the English written in the name of JHESUS MARIA, her disobedience to her parents in leaving home without their permission, why she wore male clothing, how she took communion when dressed in male clothing, and so on.

These concerns were reflected in the findings of the various University of Paris faculties, for example:

> This woman is apostate, for the hair which God gave her for a veil she has untimely cut off, and also, with the same design has rejected woman's dress and imitated the costume of men. . . . This woman is a liar and witch when she says she is sent from God, speaks with angels and saints, and yet justifies herself by no miracle or special evidence of the Scriptures.

The trial could have had two possible outcomes. Had Joan recanted, she would have been sentenced to life imprisonment. Indeed, in the churchyard of St-Ouen, under great psychological pressure from the clerics, she briefly did 'abjure':

> I, Jeanne, commonly called *The Maid*, a miserable sinner, recognising the snares of error in which I was held, and being by God's grace returned to Our Holy Mother Church, in order to show that my return is not made feignedly but with a good heart and will, I confess that I have most grievously sinned in falsely pretending to have had revelations and apparitions from God, His angels, St. Catherine and St. Margaret; in seducing others; in believing foolishly and lightly; in making superstitious divinations, in blaspheming god and His saints; in breaking the divine law, Holy Scripture and the canon laws; in wearing a dissolute, ill-shaped and immodest dress against the decency of nature, and hair cropped round like a man's, against all the modesty of womankind; also in bearing arms most presumptuously. . . .

Life imprisonment was not the outcome Bedford wanted. Nor was it the outcome, on reflection, that Joan desired. The prospect of life in prison appalled her and she hated having denied her 'voices' and her beliefs 'from fear of the fire'. So she repudiated her earlier abjuration and defiantly returned to wearing male clothing, leading the ecclesiastical court to declare that '. . . since you are fallen again – O, sorrow! – into these errors and crimes as the dog returns to his vomit, . . . we decree that you are a relapsed heretic; and . . . we denounce you as a rotten member, which, so that you shall not infect the other members of Christ, must be cast out of the unity of the Church, cut off from her body, and given over to the secular power.'

This, of course, meant given over to the English – who on 30 May 1431 burned Joan at the stake in the place du Vieux Marché in Rouen in front of a crowd of about 10,000. Bedford imagined he had achieved a propaganda victory. As Enguerrand de Monstrelet recorded, 'The King of England sent letters to the Duke of Burgundy so that the execution of justice could be published in various places by him and the other princes, and so that in future their subjects and followers might have strength to place no faith in such errors as had governed the Maid.'

To reassert English authority further, Bedford determined to have the young Henry VI also crowned King of France. Reims was in enemy hands, with an archbishop loyal to Charles VII, so Bedford settled for a coronation in Notre-Dame in Paris.

The ceremony took place in December 1431. The stage management was not entirely successful. The religious service was conducted by an English cleric, which upset the Bishop of Paris; English officers stole the chalice for which the canons of Notre-Dame then sued; a starving Paris mob invaded the banqueting hall; and 'le roi Henri II' disappointed traditional expectations of a generous bounty being distributed. Meanwhile the Duke of Burgundy was known to be negotiating with Charles VII.

A month later the ten-year-old dual monarch – King Henry VI of England and King 'Henri II' of France – crossed the Channel back to England and never returned to his French kingdom.

CHAPTER SEVEN

The French Resolution

Burgundy Changes Sides

The Duke of Burgundy had taken a solemn oath of allegiance to the English kings of France: now he wondered how to break it. Philip the Good's decision to switch sides was shaped slowly in the early 1430s. Emotionally, he still held a deep personal grudge against Charles VII for the murder of his father, John the Fearless, at Montereau. However, he could see that England was losing command of France.

The French military successes that followed Joan of Arc's liberation of Orléans had ended any serious prospect of England conquering France south of the Loire and joining its occupied territory in northern France to English Aquitaine. While Bedford led some modest military recovery in 1431, he suffered several reverses the following year. A traitor let the French into the English capital of Rouen. While the English regained command here, they lost control of Chartres a couple of months later. Bedford then staked his prestige on besieging the Marne fortress of Lagny but was outmanoeuvred and forced into a humiliating retreat.

Bedford exhausted himself at Lagny and suffered a bout of ill health. Then, at the end of 1432, his wife, Anne of Burgundy, Philip the Good's sister, died. This removed an important bond between the Duke of Burgundy and the English and Philip was offended when, only five months later, Bedford remarried into a family distrusted by the Burgundians.

Finally, with the strength of his English alliance ebbing, Philip saw a risk of Bedford negotiating an unholy alliance with Charles VII at

Burgundy's expense. Discussions between the English and the French did indeed begin at Cambrai in 1432 but were inconclusive. Philip the Good had no desire to become the isolated party in this unstable triangular relationship so he opened his own dialogue with Charles VII. Charles, of course, had long ago identified a *rapprochement* with Burgundy as the key to the expulsion of the 'Goddams' from France.

On the delicate matter of his solemn oath, Philip the Good took fresh legal advice. His chancellor, Nicolas Rolin (who might well have been in the pay of Charles VII) and other lawyers produced a variety of reinterpretations. Under the Treaty of Troyes, Charles VI of France had agreed that, on his death, the French crown should pass to his son-in-law, Henry V. In ratifying the treaty Philip the Good had therefore sworn perpetual allegiance to Henry V and his heirs, as kings of France after the death of Charles VI. But Henry V died before Charles VI and therefore never inherited the French crown himself – so he was not able to hand it on to his son, Henry VI. It could be argued, therefore, that the Treaty of Troyes did not make Philip the Good a vassal of Henry VI. If he now switched his allegiance to Charles VII, advised the sophist lawyers, he would not be breaking his oath.

However, Philip made no crude, sudden move. Instead, with the support of the papacy, he proposed summoning a peace conference. Here, with Burgundian and papal mediation, he hoped that England and France could agree to end their war. So in 1435 he hosted the grand Congress of **Arras** (see feature, p. 170–1). His clever plan was to include international observers as well as delegations from the two warring parties. Philip's prestige dwarfed that of Charles VII and the young Henry VI. Bedford had fallen ill and was now dying. So there was no other obvious host. And it was an invitation neither side would decline. The Burgundians controlled Paris and Charles VII needed Philip to switch sides if he were ever to reenter the French capital as king. The English might look askance at the idea of their chief ally posing as a peace-loving mediator but they certainly could not afford to alienate him by refusing to attend.

The Congress of Arras failed to produce peace but Philip can scarcely have been surprised by this. Now that Henry VI and Charles VII had both been crowned as rival kings of France, the prospects for any negotiated resolution of their differences were negligible. The English delegation proposed that Charles VII should retain his territory south of the Loire as a vassal of the English king of France. The French delegation insisted, as a precondition to any peace negotiations, that Henry VI drop his claim to their throne. So the English withdrew in dudgeon. A week later the Duke of Bedford died, and he was buried in Rouen Cathedral.

Philip the Good then made a separate treaty with Charles VII. Charles undertook to bring to justice the perpetrators of the murder of Philip the Good's father, and one of his courtiers apologized on his knees to Philip for this crime. This allowed Philip to feel he could recognize Charles as King of France, in return for which he received some further additions to his Burgundian territories.

As a diplomatic catalyst, to enable Philip to switch sides with advantage, the Congress of Arras had proved a successful ploy. It marked a decisive shift in the triangular relationship between Burgundy, England and France. Henry VI never did forgive the Duke of Burgundy and complained 20 years later that Philip had: 'abandoned me in my boyhood and broke all his oaths and promises to me, when I had never done him any wrong.'

Caught between War and Peace

The reaction in England to Philip the Good's betrayal, as it was seen, was initially one of indignant anger. Burgundian merchants were lynched in London. Popular feeling against the French hardened.

Objectively, however, it was hard to see how the boy King of England could ever restore the credibility of his claim to the French throne. Cardinal Beaufort, Bishop of Winchester, a legitimized son of John of Gaunt whose family wielded considerable political power throughout Henry VI's reign, became the leader of a peace faction which began to take shape in the later 1430s – and incurred the enmity of Humphrey, Duke of Gloucester as a result.

Evidence of the weakness of England's political stance was mounting. In Normandy local risings against English rule took place in Dieppe and several other nearby towns.

ARRAS

Arras was one of the biggest marketplaces in Europe in the Middle Ages. Its central features are two large cobbled squares, the Grand' Place and the place des Héros, the site of famous medieval cloth, wine and grain markets. The striped awnings of the market stalls on a Saturday make a gaudy sight to this day.

Around both squares now are tall, elegant Flemish-style town houses, with arcaded entrances and gabled roofs. They manage effortlessly to look pleasingly identical at first glance, though on closer inspection each gable and each set of windows is distinctive, and even the number of arcade arches per facade varies. While they date mainly from the seventeenth and eighteenth-centuries, the oldest house, which today serves as an attractive hotel, is fifteenth-century and was built about 30 years after Philip the Good's Congress of Arras.

The 1435 Congress was held in the ancient Benedictine abbey of Saint-Vaast. You have to use a fair amount of imagination to recreate the scene of the proud Burgundian hosts and the visiting English, French and papal representatives, whose retinues in total must have numbered several thousand, because the ancient abbey is no longer standing.

In its place is a new set of abbey buildings constructed during the eighteenth-century. Housed here now, around two cloisters, is the Fine Arts Museum, which displays some distinguished, and somewhat ghoulish, medieval funeral art as well as examples of the hanging tapestries for which Arras is famous. The adjacent cathedral is also a replacement both for an earlier abbey church and a different medieval cathedral.

Also rebuilt, but lovingly in the rich detail of the flamboyant original, is Arras Town Hall, which was destroyed by artillery in the First World War. This exuberant modern copy – with decorative arches, spiky pinnacles and gothic dormer windows, and its facade adorned by baskets of geraniums – forms the west end of the place des Héros. From the top of its 250-foot belfry you can look down on the town squares below and out at the lines of the First World War trenches in the distance to the north.

The Town Hall incorporates a Tourist Office, which presents a video 'Historama' recounting the history of Arras. It records that Joan of Arc was imprisoned here for two months before being taken to Rouen but its claim that Arras ended the Hundred Years War in 1435 glosses over a further 18 years of conflict. Arras also owns up to having been the birthplace of Robespierre, whose well-to-do house nearby can be visited.

However, the most surprising piece of history is linked to another of the Tourist Office's ticketed attractions. You can go on an underground walk through caverns originally quarried for building stone and later linked into an elaborate 20-mile network of tunnels. Their role in Arras's history includes stabling horses, housing the poor, celebrating mass illicitly during the French Revolution, storing wine, offering shelter during sieges, and providing underground communications to the Front during the First World War. Access used to be through the trap doors situated in front of each of the elegant houses surrounding the town squares: there is a great deal more to the history of Arras than first meets the eye.

More serious from England's standpoint were events in Paris. In February 1436 a Franco-Burgundian army arrived in front of the walls of the capital and blockaded it. The Parisians, who of course included Burgundians previously loyal to the English occupation, were in no mood to face a siege and the threat of starvation. The Franco-Burgundian leaders sent Marshal de l'Isle Adam to talk to the defenders on the walls:

> He showed them a general amnesty from King Charles of France, sealed with his great seal, and begged them earnestly to submit to the same King Charles at the request of the Duke of Burgundy, who was now reconciled to him, adding that in view of their constant loyalty to the duke they would remain under his governance. The Parisians listened to the gentle words of the Seigneur de l'Isle Adam and others, and it was not long before they accepted their offer and agreed together to admit them into the city. Ladders were quickly placed against the walls, and the Seigneur de l'Isle Adam climbed up into the city, followed by the bastard of Orléans and numbers of their men. A large body of the Burgundian faction and the common people gathered with them and went through the streets shouting: 'Peace! Long live the king and the Duke of Burgundy!'

The English garrison retreated to the Bastille. They were offered a safe conduct to Rouen if they agreed to evacuate Paris peacefully. They accepted and slunk out through the city gate taunted by mocking shouts from the Parisians. The following year Charles VII made a ceremonial entry into the French capital, though he did not dare to stay more than three weeks.

With first the Duke of Burgundy and now Paris having defected to Charles VII, the peace faction in England had logic on its side. However, the military situation on the ground in France was far from clear cut. It was complicated by the resurgence of bands of brigands, often former soldiers, known as *écorcheurs* (skinners), who rendered much of northern France lawless. England's veteran general, Talbot, after a spell in captivity following the Battle of Patay, was back in the field together with Bedford's successor, Richard, Duke of York. They recovered Dieppe and restored English authority in Normandy and Maine (south of Normandy).

In July 1436, shortly after the Franco-Burgundian capture of Paris, the Duke of Burgundy attacked Calais. However, he failed to blockade it effectively and was repelled first by English counterattacks and then by the arrival from England of a relief force commanded by Humphrey, Duke of Gloucester. Gloucester, who had emerged as the leader of the war faction in England, pursued the Burgundians into Flanders and returned to England as the hero who had punished the perfidious Duke.

Talbot then had a further string of victories: at Ris near Rouen, at Ivry, and at Pontoise, just outside Paris, where he put Marshal de l'Isle Adam to flight. The Duke of York was replaced for a period by the Earl of Warwick, who sent Talbot north to Le Crotoy on the Somme where again the Burgundians were defeated. It was Talbot's strength in the field that made Charles VII so cautious about remaining in Paris in 1437.

As the war and peace factions took shape around him, Henry VI, now in his late teens, started to take a more personal role in English government. He was certainly no warrior. Though he was to reign for nearly 40 years, many historians would say he was no king. He was gentle and pious, worshipped frequently, dressed simply – sometimes wearing a hair shirt beneath his ceremonial robes – and was merciful to a fault. He had none of Edward III's or Henry V's drive to assert his claim to the French throne, though he believed he was by right entitled to it. He had no political skills or judgment. Though averse to war, he was incapable of planning and conducting an effective peace negotiation.

In 1438 Charles VII attacked Aquitaine, but without much success. In 1439, therefore, both sides were willing to consider peace. An Anglo-French conference was organized near Gravelines, not far from Calais. Henry VI remained inflexible on his claim to be king of France, however, so the war continued.

The ineffectual nature of English policy was illustrated by the release of Charles, Duke of Orléans, who had been captured at Agincourt and held in captivity in England for a quarter of a century. Henry V, as he lay dying in 1422, had advised against ever releasing Orléans and, throughout the 1430s, Humphrey of Gloucester continued to champion that view. Beaufort and the peace faction, on the other hand, argued that Orléans might be able to broker a settlement between England and France.

In 1440, with this object in mind, Henry VI agreed to free Orléans. At a solemn ceremony in Westminster Abbey, from which Gloucester stormed out, Orléans undertook to do his best to arrange peace. However, Charles VII took relatively little interest in this English initiative and, indeed, it was the Duke of Burgundy who raised Orléans's ransom money. Orléans returned to France to live privately, without being in a position to advance Henry's quest for peace.

The Truce of Tours

In the early 1440s the war faction in England steadily lost ground. Humphrey of Gloucester, whose advice over Orléans's release had been so conspicuously defied, suffered a further blow to his prestige on account of his wife.

It may be recalled that, after his somewhat farcical expedition to the Low Countries in support of Jacqueline of Hainault in 1421, Gloucester had taken up with one of her ladies-in-waiting. This was Eleanor Cobham, by whom he had two children before marrying her in 1431. Now, in 1441, Eleanor was found guilty of sorcery. She had made a wax image of Henry VI and melted it, willing his death so that Gloucester, the king's uncle and heir, might inherit the throne. She was made to walk the streets of London in her shift for three days, as public penance, before beginning a sentence of life imprisonment.

In France, Talbot, under the Duke of York's command once again, continued to campaign energetically and drove Charles VII away from besieging Pontoise, near Paris. But as soon as Talbot returned to Normandy Charles VII renewed the siege, deploying his new artillery expert, Jean Bureau, whose cannon soon demolished the Pontoise defences. Charles VII had now made Paris safe from any further serious threat.

In 1442 Charles VII invaded Aquitaine and threatened Bordeaux. Beaufort's nephew was put in charge of England's military response. He landed a fresh English army in Cherbourg and marched south towards

Aquitaine. However, he proved incompetent and, after some fruitless activity on the borders of Brittany, returned in humiliation to England, to die shortly afterwards.

With the failure of a war strategy, the peace faction gained the upper hand. It was led now by William de la Pole, Earl (and later Duke) of Suffolk. Suffolk had fought in France during Joan of Arc's time and had been captured at Jargeau. Having paid his own ransom, he returned to England to become the custodian and friend of Charles of Orléans and a protégé of Cardinal Beaufort's. As such, he was an enemy of Gloucester's, and he was one of the commissioners appointed to investigate Eleanor of Cobham's sorcery.

By 1444 Henry VI and his Council had taken the decision to seek a French marriage for the king as the foundation for a new relationship of Anglo-French peace. Charles VII's niece, Margaret of Anjou, had been identified by discreet soundings as a suitable candidate, close enough a relation to the French king for Henry VI's purposes but not so close, from Charles VII's point of view, as to risk compounding English claims to the throne of France in a later generation. Suffolk was asked to lead an embassy to France to seek a truce and secure the marriage.

Suffolk was initially apprehensive about this. He was convinced that England needed peace but he was also conscious of the weakness of the English negotiating position and of the risk that, if he did have to make concessions which proved unpopular, Gloucester and the war faction would cast him as the villain. He asked for an undertaking that, should the mission fail, no blame would attach to him.

Suffolk called on his old friend Charles of Orléans, then made his way to **Tours** (see feature), the family home of René, Duke of Anjou, Margaret's father. Charles VII also arrived in Tours, followed by a Burgundian delegation, so three-way peace negotiations could restart. Charles VII had no need to make any concessions and had no intention of concluding a peace settlement unless the English in effect surrendered. Suffolk did manage to secure agreement to a two-year truce and to the proposed marriage, provided Margaret renounced all claims to her father's possessions.

In the presence of Charles VII and the leading French royalty and nobles, the betrothal took place in the Basilica of Saint-Martin in

TOURS

Tours has invested in making itself attractive – as the willow-lined walk along the Loire, the flags decorating the Pont Wilson, the pedestrian suspension bridge and, above all, the renovation of the old city all testify.

Apparently the city was always enterprising. In 397 when Saint Martin (originally a young Roman soldier who slashed his cloak to give half to a beggar, became a Christian and was later bishop here) died near Poitiers, the people of Tours were quick to retrieve his body. Pilgrimages to the tomb of Saint Martin became the foundation for Tours' growth.

The massive 'ancien' Basilica of Saint-Martin, built between the eleventh and thirteenth-centuries, was sadly destroyed by a combination of the Wars of Religion and the French Revolution. It was here that the betrothal of Margaret of Anjou to Henry VI (represented by the Duke of Suffolk) took place in the presence of Charles VII in 1444.

Today only two, still imposing, remnants of the old Basilica stand – the Tour Charlemagne from the north transept and, now a couple of streets away, the Tour d'Horloge from the south-west corner. 'Dinosaur footprints' along the Rue des Halles mark the bases of the old columns, underlining the scale. Nearby is the nineteenth-century 'nouvelle' Basilica designed by Victor Laloux, who was also the architect for the Gare d'Orsay in Paris (now the Musée d'Orsay) and Tours's grandiose Hôtel de Ville.

Around Saint-Martin is the old town of Tours, centred on the place Plumereau, attractively pedestrianized and dotted with well-preserved medieval houses. The rue Briçonnet includes both a thirteenth-century facade and the late fifteenth-century Flemish-style Maison de Tristan.

After Margaret of Anjou's betrothal service at Saint-Martin, the guests repaired to the Abbey of Saint-Julian for the celebrations. The abbey too has suffered over the centuries. The gothic church of Saint-Julian, with a romanesque tower from an earlier construction, has survived being used as a stable during the French Revolution. Around the adjacent ruined cloister are two museums occupying the old cellars, dormitory and chapter house – a whimsical Musée des Vins de Touraine and an institution called the Musée de Compagnonnage. This is devoted to craftsmanship, as fostered from the Middle Ages onwards by guilds whose curious, and at times secretive, history is recounted here.

Tours's third major religious edifice, which now has undisputed pride of place, is its twin-towered gothic cathedral. Its noteworthy features include its stained-glass windows, the early sixteenth-century tomb of the children of Charles VIII, the cloister and the Renaissance staircase there leading up to the Salle des Archives.

The Fine Arts Museum looks onto a square named after Gregory of Tours, who was bishop here in the sixteenth-century. In the rue Colbert a plaque marks the house of Joan of Arc's armourer. With all this history, you might have considered visiting the 'Historial' display, which the guide books say is in the Château, but this has now closed, leaving, incongruously, an aquarium. The Château itself is part medieval and part eighteenth-century.

Charles VII's son, Louis XI, was particularly fond of residing in Tours.

Tours. At the centre of the ceremony were the 15-year-old Margaret of Anjou, the prospective bride, and Suffolk, acting as proxy for Henry VI.

Suffolk was greeted on his return with effusive gratitude by Henry VI, who naively hoped that the truce would lead in due course to a proper peace treaty. The following year Suffolk was sent back to France for the wedding. This took place in Nancy in Lorraine. Like the betrothal, it was preceded by negotiations and there were rumours – probably false – that the French were only willing to bring Margaret from Anjou to Nancy if Suffolk conceded the English-held territory of Maine (bordering Normandy and Brittany) to her father.

Suffolk stood in for Henry VI once more at the wedding celebration and then conducted his new queen back to England to meet her real husband. After a further marriage ceremony at Titchfield she was crowned in Westminster Abbey. Margaret of Anjou and Suffolk had by then formed a strong political bond and a commitment to Henry VI's goal of turning the Truce of Tours into a permanent peace settlement.

Queen Margaret, though young, easily dominated her guileless husband and, of course, retained her affection for France. During the Anglo-French diplomatic discussions, which continued in England in the summer and autumn of 1445, she urged Henry to surrender Maine to her father, on the grounds that it would help promote an agreement. In December that year Henry VI wrote to Charles VII personally, agreeing to surrender Le Mans and the surrounding county of Maine, in response to 'our most dear and well-beloved companion the queen, who has requested us to do this many times.' Having been offered this concession, Charles VII then insisted that it be implemented before he would agree to an extension of the truce, let alone to Henry VI's proposal for a personal meeting of the two kings.

Implementation would not be easy. Suffolk calculated that he would first need to neutralize the residual war faction. In February 1447 Humphrey of Gloucester was arrested for treason. Shortly afterwards, he died. Rumours circulated that Suffolk had had him murdered but it is more likely that Gloucester suffered a stroke. The Duke of York was recalled from France and, much against his will, sent to Ireland. His role in France as Lieutenant-General and Governor (in effect the position

Bedford had held as Regent) was entrusted to yet another member of the Beaufort family, Edmund, Duke of Somerset. Charles VII agreed to an extension of the truce provided Maine was handed over, so Somerset was given the invidious task of transferring it.

Charles VII Knows what he Wants

Charles VII took a very pragmatic view of the truce. Cast as a hesitant weakling in the legend of Joan of Arc, in maturity he displayed a clear resolve to establish the integrity of his French kingdom.

Having returned to Paris, he based his government there – but the transition was not an easy one. Paris and much of northern France had been ruled by the Burgundians. Charles had no desire to become dependent on the Duke of Burgundy, whom he regarded, not unreasonably, as opportunistic. He therefore needed steadily to replace government officials loyal to Philip the Good with officials loyal to himself. Though he now resided in Paris, he continued to rely on a Bourges clique with whom he had built up a close relationship of trust – and in which his mistress, Agnès Sorel, was influential.

Charles had to suppress a conspiracy, known as the 'Praguerie' (a reference to a topical revolt in Bohemia), supported by a number of leading figures he had thought he could trust. Even his own son, the Dauphin Louis, aged 16 and already keen to reign, was involved.

So, although Charles VII's position at the time of the truce was considerably stronger than Henry VI's, the French king had much to accomplish within his own realm before he could be ready for an all-out assault on the English. His two priorities were ample government finance and a strong royal army.

During his years in Bourges, Charles had been desperately short of money for much of the time. In 1438 he appointed as his *argentier* (paymaster-general) a self-made merchant called Jacques Coeur, who built up an astonishingly rich business in the 1440s. He was France's largest ship-owner and traded from one end of the Mediterranean to the other; he manufactured arms and armour; he mined silver; and he acted as the king's tax farmer. Immensely rich himself, Coeur looked after the king's cash needs. Charles and his officials also overhauled

France's tax system, shifting taxation onto a more permanent basis. So by the late 1440s Charles could afford to finance a new military campaign.

In parallel, he built up a full-time professional army. By royal edict he created companies of soldiers who were well-armed and properly paid, so that they would not disperse at the end of each campaign to become brigands. A further edict obliged every parish to support an archer, so that a body of 8,000 archers could be summoned in the event of need. As an incentive to belong to this 'territorial army', these archers were exempted from tax. The other major military reform was to develop an artillery – and here Charles was served by Jean Bureau who, assisted by his brother Gaspard, proved a master at deploying modern cannon effectively in battle.

While France was using the truce to prepare for a resumption of war, English policy was a muddle. English troop numbers had been reduced and pay arrears had triggered some mutinies. While Henry VI wanted to surrender Maine, the garrisons there resisted the idea. Only when Charles VII pointedly besieged Le Mans did the English finally leave Maine in 1448.

Instead of just withdrawing the English garrisons into Normandy, Somerset sent some of his troops to occupy two fortresses on the Brittany-Maine border. The Duke of Brittany objected and Charles VII, who regarded the duke as a vassal of France, supported him. Somerset replied that Charles had no standing in the matter, since Brittany was an English fief.

Then in March 1449 Somerset (and perhaps Suffolk) authorized an Aragonese mercenary called François de Surienne to mount a surprise attack on the Breton town of **Fougères** (see feature, p. 182–3). According to one chronicler, it was no trivial incident:

> Sir Francis (de Surienne) was accompanied by six hundred or seven hundred men-at-arms, some French-speaking and some English, who did all possible damage in the city, killing many, taking some prisoner, destroying churches, raping women, and seizing all the wealth they could lay their hands on. Not content with this, they overran the duchy, where they killed or took prisoners, ravaged the countryside and generally did every exploit that is customary in war.

While Somerset might have needed some local act of revenge to bolster morale after the humiliation of the withdrawal from Maine, this military adventure sat oddly with the English policy of trying to appease the French into agreeing a peace settlement. It may well have been part of some elaborate English plot to support the younger brother of the Duke of Brittany against his sibling who was thought to be too sympathetic to Charles VII – but, if so, it was ineffective. The English did nothing to follow up this isolated act of aggression and, a few months later, de Surienne surrendered the town.

Charles VII could fairly portray the attack on Fougères as a blatant breach of the truce. He had been preparing for a new onslaught against the English occupying forces and he now had his opportunity. In 1449 he threw 30,000 troops into an attack on the English strongholds of Normandy.

The Fall of Normandy

The retention of Normandy was probably, by then, England's highest priority – given the difficulty of re-establishing the plausibility of Henry VI's claim to be the true king of France. But Somerset's disposition of England's scattered and demoralized forces failed to reflect this.

Across the province, English military power crumbled. Dunois, the Bastard of Orléans, led the main French army up the Seine, capturing Verneuil, Mantes and Vernon (see Map 15, p. 184). Meanwhile the Constable of France, Arthur de Richemont, another veteran from Joan of Arc's campaigns, led a Franco-Breton force that subjugated the lower Cotentin.

In October 1449, accompanied by the French king, Dunois and Jean Bureau arrived in front of Rouen. Inside were Somerset and Talbot and an English garrison of about 1,200 men.

The French army dug trenches and settled down for a siege, with Bureau's artillery pounding the city walls. But it was the citizens of Rouen who took charge of events. The folk memory of Henry V's cruel siege of their city remained strong. The Rouennais did not propose to starve for the sake of the English. They opened the gates to

FOUGERES

Fougères is a town of granite and slate, built to withstand attack. It is still visibly divided into the three traditional areas of a fortified medieval town – the suburbs outside the defending walls, the commercial centre within them, and the inner sanctum of a castle. Large-scale, well-preserved, and with fairy-tale turrets and battlements, Fougères's castle is spectacular. It too subdivides into three – an outer area for assessing strangers, a residential inner courtyard, and a military keep.

Originally a wooden structure burned down by Henry II, the massive stone castle that stands today was built between the thirteenth and the fifteenth-centuries. The thick horseshoe-shaped towers, designed to defy artillery attack, were built after the Hundred Years War – but most of what you see is the actual citadel that Bertrand du Guesclin attacked in 1373 and François de Surienne raided in 1449.

To appreciate the castle fully, it is worth viewing it from the promontory on the cliff, the other side of the River Nançon. From the terraced gardens with attractive water features in front of the Church of St-Léonard, you can look across the valley and take in the full breadth and strength of the castle. Perched on a bed of hard rock with the river meandering round its base into its moat, it is a classic example of military architecture.

If you then descend towards the castle, you can walk through the narrow medieval streets around the place du Marchix along to Porte Notre-Dame, the last surviving gate in the town wall. Entering the castle, you see a group of four wooden water-wheels, driven by a millstream from the moat, which, together with drawbridge, form the main feature of the outer area. Inside the residential courtyard are the remains of a chapel and a set of pillars, which once supported a splendid banqueting hall. Within the keep you can climb the Mélusine and Gobelins towers into which besieged garrisons could retreat as a last refuge. Only by taking the defenders by complete surprise, in breach of the truce, could de Surienne have captured Fougères so swiftly.

Adjacent is the church of Saint-Sulpice, with an unusual slate spire and a wooden panelled interior. Up the hill in the main town centre are a fourteenth-century slate belfry and the birthplace of the eighteenth-century Marquis de la Rouërie, of whom there's a suitably dashing statue. The Marquis, a veteran of the American War of Independence, led a Breton rebellion against the French Revolution. He died in 1793 but the partisan movement he founded, Les Chouans, fought on until 1804, and featured later in the novels of Victor Hugo and Honoré de Balzac.

Fougères is proud of its writers. If you are keen, you can follow the Circuit Littéraire and find all 25 of the plaques with quotes from famous authors who lived in, or wrote about, the town.

There was a time when Fougères paid less attention to enticing tourists. From the mid-nineteenth-century onwards the principal industry was shoe-making. The castle meanwhile, having served as a prison for a period, had passed into private hands. Perhaps foreseeing that shoe-making might not prosper forever, the town, aided by the state, shrewdly bought back the castle in 1892.

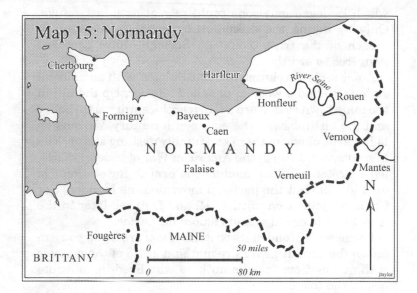

Map 15: Normandy

the French, forcing Somerset, Talbot and the English garrison to retreat hurriedly into the castle, without foodstocks.

Somerset attempted to negotiate an amnesty that would allow the English to leave safely. Charles VII refused, on the grounds that Somerset had occupied the castle and attempted to prevent Rouen from surrendering. He would only concede safe passage if the English agreed to surrender several other towns in Normandy and leave Talbot as a hostage.

Somerset resisted briefly but, when the French army began to besiege the castle, he capitulated. He agreed terms with a delegation of French negotiators, which allowed him, his wife and most of the English to leave but

> Within a year they were to pay to the king the sum of fifty thousand crowns, and six thousand to those with whom the treaty had been made. They further promised to make a faithful settlement of all that they owed to the innkeepers, townsfolk, merchants and anyone else in the city. The Duke of Somerset and his companions also gave assurances that they would deliver to

the King of France or his representatives the castle of Arques, the town of Caudebec, the castles of Tancarville and Lillebonne and the towns of Honfleur and Montivilliers. Apart from his written assurances, the Duke of Somerset left as hostages for their fulfilment Lord Talbot and seven other English noblemen.

In the event, the commander of Honfleur refused to obey these humiliating terms and Talbot was left in captivity. Somerset withdrew to Caen.

Over the following months the French continued their Norman reconquest. Towns surrendered readily, sometimes with spontaneous risings against the English occupation forces, sometimes with persuasion by Jean Bureau's artillery. Harfleur, Henry V's first colony in Normandy, fell at the end of 1449.

Back in England, Suffolk struggled to cope with the failure of English diplomacy, the collapse of the English military occupation, and the return of the dispossessed, impoverished and furious English settlers, many of whom had lived in France for most of their lives. He despatched a relief army under the command of Sir Thomas Kyriel but Kyriel's troops mutinied in Portsmouth, robbed the locals and delayed the expedition for several months.

In March 1450 Kyriel finally landed at Cherbourg with only 2,500 men. Lingering in the Cotentin, he persuaded Somerset to send him such reinforcements as could be put together in Normandy, bringing his army's strength up to about 4,000. He then marched to the relief of Bayeux (see Map 15).

On 15 April 1450 Kyriel's army was camped near the village of Formigny, on the road between the Cotentin and Bayeux. He was overtaken by a pursuing French army under the command of the Count of Clermont. Although he had fewer men than Kyriel, Clermont decided to attack. He also sent word to call for help from de Richemont who had an additional French force further to the south.

Kyriel arranged his army in the Agincourt formation to face Clermont (see Map 16). The English archers inflicted significant casualties on the French – and when Clermont brought a couple of

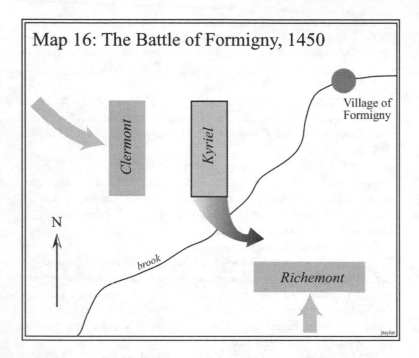

Map 16: The Battle of Formigny, 1450

cannon into action the English charged out and captured them. Kyriel must have thought the day was his.

Then Richemont arrived from the south, heading for the English flank, with another 1,200 French troops. Kyriel deployed his own force in an arc in an attempt to face Clermont and Richemont simultaneously, but Clermont exploited his stretched formation and Richemont's cavalry charge was unstoppable. Kyriel himself was captured. Most of his troops were killed. The Battle of Formigny, commemorated today only by an obscure roadside monument, effectively ended the English occupation of Normandy.

Bayeux swiftly fell and the French then laid siege to Caen, where the Duke of Somerset represented what was left of Henry VI's authority in France. Bombarded by Bureau's cannon, Somerset again surrendered and this time was allowed to withdraw to Calais.

Nearby Falaise continued to withstand attack, but the English garrison there shrewdly negotiated the town's surrender in return for the release of Talbot. Charles VII agreed to this but made it a condition that Talbot, now an old man, took an oath never again to wear armour against the French.

That left only the port of Cherbourg, where the English still had a garrison, to which Richemont and Bureau turned next:

> The town received such a heavy battering from cannon and bombards that the like had never been seen before. There were even bombards situated on the sea shore between high and low tide, which were loaded with boulders; although they were under water when the tide was in, they were covered over with greased skins so that the sea did no harm to their powder, and as soon as the tide went out the cannoneers removed the coverings and continued firing into the town, to the great astonishment of the English, who had never seen anything like it.

In August 1450, just over a year after Charles VII had launched his attack on English Normandy, the last English garrison there surrendered.

The Harsh Price of Defeat

The scale and speed of the English defeats in Normandy shocked England. The English had basked for several decades in the memory of Henry V's glorious victory at Agincourt, reinforced by the stories handed down of the Black Prince's capture of the French king and Edward III's triumph at Crécy. More recent setbacks had seemed minor by comparison and neither the English court nor the wider country was emotionally prepared for the humiliating disasters of 1450.

Increasing numbers of refugees were returning from France to England with only whatever personal possessions they could carry. Reportedly, more than 6,000 refugees reached England in the two months of July and August alone. They petitioned the king for financial assistance but received none. The rumour that Somerset had received compensation for his losses in the surrender of Maine aggravated their bitter anger.

The defeats were blamed on the king himself and on his military and political appointees – especially the Beauforts. The military leader responsible was Somerset, a Beaufort. The political leader was Suffolk, who had been a Beaufort protégé and whose son had married into the Beaufort family. The Beauforts were Henry VI's relatives. The king was the great-grandson of John of Gaunt, Duke of Lancaster, through Gaunt's first marriage, while the Beauforts were the legitimized off-spring of Gaunt and Katherine Swynford, a family governess and Gaunt's mistress whom he finally married as his third wife. During the preceding decades, this Lancastrian clan had constituted the peace faction. It was now widely blamed for having betrayed the country. Henry VI's French queen was also seen as a sinister power behind the throne.

The Lancastrian family reputation never recovered. It could too easily be contrasted with that of the Duke of York, a descendant of John of Gaunt's younger brother, Edmund Duke of York, and a former ally of Humphrey of Gloucester's war faction. Helped hugely by Talbot, York had achieved a sound military record in France but had been removed from command there to make way for Somerset. The seeds of the later War of the Roses, between the House of Lancaster and the House of York, started to germinate in this climate of defeat.

More immediately, popular discontent with the king and his government came to a head with a rebellion in Kent in the summer of 1450. It was led by Jack Cade, who may have been a former murderer, had probably done some military service in Normandy, and now claimed royal descent. He recruited a large following and led a march on London. The rebels complained that the king had given away so much territory that he now had to rely on excessively heavy taxes on the English people, that the tax administration and the judiciary were corrupt, and that those responsible for losing Normandy were traitors who should be punished.

In response Henry VI sent his unpopular Treasurer, Lord Saye, to the Tower. Meanwhile the royal council despatched troops to disperse the rebels but failed to send enough, so Cade successfully rallied his supporters while Henry VI fled to Warwickshire.

The rebellion spread briefly throughout much of southern England

and Cade entered London in style. There he freed all the prisoners in the Marshalsea, captured the Tower of London, and beheaded Lord Saye in a tavern. The rebels then quarrelled among themselves, were set upon by government troops, and, after heavy fighting, retreated. Cade attempted to flee in disguise but was caught and killed. His head was displayed on London Bridge, where much of the fighting had taken place, facing Kent.

A mob attacked Somerset when he returned to England later that year and ransacked his house. Henry VI appointed him to serve in Calais. When Parliament called for Somerset's banishment, Henry initially ignored it, then put him briefly under arrest, and finally, encouraged by the Queen, brought him back into power in England.

However, Henry failed to protect Suffolk. Accused by Parliament of treason, Suffolk was imprisoned in the Tower. The case against him included securing the release of Charles of Orléans, surrendering Maine, making unworthy appointments, and failing to strengthen the English forces in France. As an ally of the Beauforts, a friend of the Queen, the leading figure in the king's government, and the architect of Somerset's appointment, he was politically very vulnerable. But the animosity towards Suffolk went further: there were allegations that he had behaved corruptly, taken bribes from France, made illicit deals, and betrayed English military secrets. There was even a charge that he was conspiring to seize the throne for his son on the basis of the latter's marriage into the Beaufort family.

In reality Suffolk was probably a man of integrity, loyally trying to pursue peace in a situation where English victory was no longer a realistic expectation, but who misread Charles VII's intentions and then appointed an incompetent English commander. His political judgement had proved disastrous but the allegations of treason were almost certainly misplaced.

Seeking to protect him from execution, Henry VI agreed to Suffolk's banishment for five years. On 1 May 1450, having reiterated his innocence, Suffolk therefore boarded a ship for Calais where he hoped he could live in safety. Not far out at sea he was intercepted by a ship called *Nicholas of the Tower*, which on someone's orders (possibly the Duke of York's), had been lying in wait. Suffolk was taken on board. The next day his attackers took him off in a rowing boat and made him lay his head on the gunwhale. Then, with six strokes of a rusty sword, they cut through his neck.

The Loss of Aquitaine

At the heart of the earlier Anglo-French conflict during the fourteenth century, Aquitaine had been more of a military backwater under the Lancastrians. While the armies of Henry V, Bedford and Joan of Arc had been battling across northern France, life in Bordeaux and the surrounding area had continued with far less disruption. The historic turning-points in the Anglo-French-Burgundian relationship had little immediate impact. The English were not seen as a hated occupying force. After three centuries, stretching back to the time of Eleanor of Aquitaine, an English presence was normal.

The border areas of English Aquitaine were more unstable. Charles VII had invaded in 1438, made some conquests and lost most of them the following year. He attacked again in 1442, but otherwise, pre-occupied with France north of the Loire, he simply encouraged his local followers in Aquitaine to continue local wars of attrition. Strongholds like the **Château de Castelnaud** (see feature, p. 192–3) changed allegiance several times in the ebb and flow of local fighting.

In 1450 after expelling the English from Normandy, Charles VII began a full-scale assault on Aquitaine. One army advanced along the valley of the River Adour towards Bayonne, while another captured Bergerac and advanced on Bordeaux (see Map 17). A planned relief expedition from England was held up by financial and logistical problems and never set sail.

In 1451 Dunois marched south at the head of a larger French army, including Jean Bureau and his artillery. Boosted by improvements in gunpowder techniques, artillery was now a significant factor in warfare – whether used in sieges or in prepared defensive positions on the battlefield – and the French had been quick to exploit its potential. Bureau trained his guns on the defensive forts surrounding Bordeaux. A combined French and Spanish fleet in the Gironde reinforced the siege.

Despairing of the arrival of the English relief force, the Bordeaux

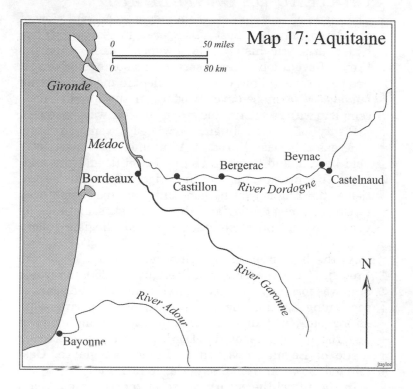

Map 17: Aquitaine

garrison surrendered and Dunois entered the city in triumph in June 1451. Bayonne fell in August. Charles VII now controlled all the main English strongholds in the duchy. It had been another swift conquest.

However, the French military victory here was much more precarious than in Normandy. Whereas Charles VII had in many respects been seen as a liberator in Normandy, here he was regarded as a conqueror. The local leaders of Aquitaine had enjoyed substantial autonomy under English rule and Charles, while not punitive at this stage, did not trust them. He appointed a Breton as his governor in Aquitaine and made Jean Bureau mayor of Bordeaux. Moreover, the wine trade with England, which had flourished in the 1440s and was the main foundation of Bordeaux's prosperity, now collapsed. In 1452

CHATEAU DE CASTELNAUD

The castle of Castelnaud commands a wonderful view of the Dordogne valley, east of Bergerac, in Périgord. It has had a dramatic history. Its low point came after the French Revolution, when it served as a stone pit. Today it has been restored not only as a splendid medieval castle but also as a museum of warfare in the Middle Ages, complete with reconstructed stone-slinging war machines.

Plenty of stone slinging obviously went on here. Whereas the coastal area of Aquitaine was consistently held by England between the mid-twelfth and the mid-fifteenth-centuries, up here in Périgord the eastern frontier of the English duchy constantly shifted. Sometimes territory changed allegiance by conquest, sometimes by peace treaty. And Castelnaud changed allegiance more than most.

At the beginning of the Hundred Years War it was French. Under the Treaty of Brétigny in 1360, the whole area was formally transferred to England. In the years of continuing fighting thereafter, most of the surrounding strongholds, including Castelnaud's long-standing rival just the other side of the Dordogne, the neighbouring castle of Beynac, reverted to French allegiance. Castelnaud, however, remained loyal to England.

In the fifteenth-century phase of the Hundred Years War, the English lost and recaptured Castelnaud five times. It was in English hands in 1442 during the closing stages of the war, as French control was expanding and consolidating all around.

Then France's King Charles VII issued this order to his local supporters, including the lord of Beynac: 'We, Charles, by the grace of God King of France, salute you. Not being able ourselves to put under obedience our villages of Bergerac, Castelnaud ... and several other places which are held by our ancient enemies and adversaries the English, we give power hereby to our dear friends ...

Assemble all manner of people and provide supplies, artillery, labourers, carpenters and masons, paying them all a reasonable sum, to lay siege to these said places and put them back under our allegiance.'

The lord of Beynac and his colleagues needed no further bidding. In the castle today, a display that the French term a 'diaporama' – a model, animated dramatically with light and sound – tells the story of the ensuing battle, which ended with the English in Castelnaud surrendering in return for their lives and 400 pieces of gold.

There is plenty more to the story, both before the Hundred Years War and later during the French Wars of Religion. The castle of Castelnaud has layers of construction from the different eras of its history: a thirteenth-century donjon and surrounding walls; a lower courtyard from the late fifteenth-century; a sixteenth-century artillery tower; and an outer courtyard completed in the seventeenth-century.

The displays of battle-axes, swords, halberds, crossbows, helmets, armour, catapults and then early cannon and firearms are complemented by videos explaining how the evolution of weapons of attack determined the most effective forms of defence and vice versa. Castelnaud has become a good family museum.

Bordeaux therefore despatched a secret mission to England promising that, if England would send a relief army, the local population would rise against the French.

Somerset, who was briefly in power at that point, saw an opportunity to retrieve some shreds of his military reputation after the disasters of Normandy. He turned to Talbot, now white-haired and in his seventies, to lead the relief expedition.

The French picked up some intelligence of his preparations but assumed he would invade Normandy, so Talbot and 3,000 English troops made a surprise landing in Médoc in October 1452. True to their promise, the people of Bordeaux threw out the French garrison, opened their gates, and welcomed Talbot enthusiastically. The surrounding towns and castles did likewise.

Charles VII was furious, both with Talbot who had been released under an oath never again to wear armour against France, and with the Bordelais on whom he now swore vengeance: 'It is our intention, with the help of Our Creator, to have the town, and all those in it and their goods, placed at our disposal, in order to punish their bodies according to their deserts for having broken their oaths and expressions of loyalty to us, so that it would be an example to others and a reminder in the future.'

Charles spent the winter raising another army which he directed to attack the English-held towns along the Dordogne. Jean Bureau led the force, which laid siege to **Castillon** (see feature, p. 196–7). Talbot meanwhile had received further reinforcements, under the command of his son, Lord de Lisle, so they ventured out of Bordeaux in response to an appeal from the citizens of Castillon.

Some 30 miles from Bordeaux, Castillon lay on the Dordogne River and its little tributary, the Lidoire. Jean Bureau had established his artillery between the Dordogne and the Lidoire, with the latter shielding him from an attack from the rear (see Map 18). He had about 300 guns, which he protected with an elaborate set of earthworks fortified by tree trunks.

At dawn on 17 July 1453, Talbot arrived with a small advance force ahead of his main army. He swiftly overcame a troop of French archers in the priory outside the town and started to take stock of the French

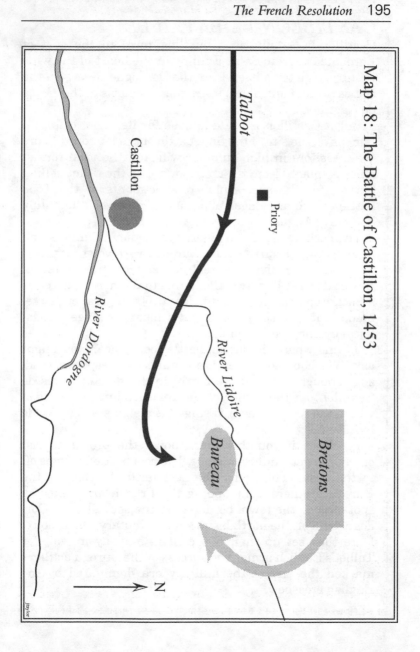

Map 18: The Battle of Castillon, 1453

CASTILLON-LA-BATAILLE

Castillon-la-Bataille is a bustling town to the east of Bordeaux, close to Saint-Emilion in the heart of the wine country. The town itself is on the Dordogne River. On the slopes around and above it are the vineyards of the 'Côtes de Castillon'.

But if Castillon is *quite* famous for its wine, it is *very* famous as the site of the final battle of the Hundred Years War. Visitors in high summer will find the local tourist office displaced from the main square by the ticket-selling bureau for the spectacular re-enactments of the 1453 battle, which are staged about a dozen times in late July and early August.

The cardboard cut-out figures of medieval knights and infantry, which surround the bureau, warn you that this is no academic activity. A real château on the hilltop of Belves de Castillon, two kilometres to the north, serves as a backdrop. And in a field below it 500 actors, 50 horsemen, lights, music, cannon and a narrator stage a theatrical evening performance.

'Is this where the actual battle took place?' you might ask. 'We hope so' comes the commercial response. And, sure enough, if you drive north up the hill to Belves de Castillon, on the corner of the road leading to the field where the re-enactment is staged is a sign saying 'Site de la Bataille'.

However, if you then hunt down the proper tourist office, you get a different story. The real battlefield was off to the east. Looking for the best natural defences, the Bureau brothers commanding the French army chose a spot outside the town, bordered on the south by the Dordogne and on the north by its small tributary, the Lidoire. Here they set up their 300 cannon and lay in wait for Talbot's English army. The success of the Bureau artillery marked the end of the military era dominated by the English crossbow.

The other delicate question is which side the people of Castillon were on: they had, after all, belonged to English Aquitaine for three centuries and they did warn Talbot when the French army arrived outside their town.

The tourist literature diplomatically states: 'Paradoxically the Castillonais took little or no part in this important event, which history will always remember. Within the shelter of their walls they were able to follow the cavalry charges, hear the crash of the cannon and noise of battle almost like spectators at a drama, of whose manifold and distant repercussions they could have had no inkling.'

Talbot's death on the battlefield is, however, honoured. Castillon's main street is called the avenue John Talbot. Further afield, in the Haut-Médoc area north of Bordeaux, the Château Talbot produces a decent claret. And at the site of the battlefield itself, up a rose-lined path beside a vineyard stands a pillar with a statue of the Virgin on top and, at its base, a plaque commemorating 'le Général J. Talbot'.

positions. He learned of Bureau's artillery base, around which a cloud of dust was now seen. Talbot inferred from this, or was mistakenly informed, that Bureau had decided to retreat. So, without waiting for all his own troops to arrive, Talbot charged off expecting to harry the fleeing French columns.

Instead he encountered Bureau's prepared defensive position, which he proceeded to attack. Riding a white pony, dressed in a crimson gown, and with no armour (to honour, quite literally, the oath he had taken when released from Falaise) he ordered the newly arrived detachments of his main army into battle.

Bureau's guns mowed the English down. Then a Breton cavalry troop charged in from the flank to help complete the slaughter. Talbot himself fell when a cannonball hit his horse and a French soldier killed him with a battle-axe. His son, Lord de Lisle, was also killed. The English army was annihilated.

The Battle of Castillon in effect concluded the war. The victorious French army advanced to Bordeaux, capturing other towns en route, and laid siege to the capital, and last surviving outpost, of English Aquitaine. The Bordelais resisted but, with the Gironde blockaded and no prospect of a further English expedition, their position was hopeless. They surrendered in October 1453. Charles VII banished the local leaders, exacted a fine of 100,000 gold crowns, and made Jean Bureau mayor of Bordeaux for life.

Back in England King Henry VI went mad, much as his French grandfather Charles VI had done. It was a fitting end to the Hundred Years War.

Epilogue

Aftermath

The fact that the Hundred Years War was over was only decided by posterity – as indeed was the idea that the conflict that flared up and died down several times between 1337 and 1453 should be termed 'the Hundred Years War'. No peace treaty finally to end, or resolve, the English kings' claim to the French throne followed the battles of Formigny and Castillon. The English continued to occupy Calais. Charles VII concluded he could not evict them from this last English outpost in France. Nor could he be sure that England would not attempt a further invasion of either Normandy or Aquitaine.

Having so successfully exploited baronial conflict in France in the past, however, England now descended into civil war itself. Henry VI's bout of madness, following so closely on the military disasters his government had suffered, reduced the Lancastrian monarchy's standing in the country to danger point. Queen Margaret gave birth to Henry's son and heir in 1453 but, during Henry's spell of madness, Richard Duke of York became Protector of the Realm. He imprisoned Somerset in the Tower.

At the end of 1454 Henry VI recovered, at any rate temporarily, and released Somerset. At St Albans, in 1455, the first of many battles between the House of Lancaster, whose emblem was the red rose, and the House of York, symbolized by the white rose, followed. Somerset was killed on the battlefield.

Having failed in their wars against the French, the English nobility spent the next generation fighting one another in the Wars of the

Roses. In 1460 the Yorkists captured Henry VI. The Lancastrians then captured and beheaded Richard Duke of York. Henry VI was released but the Lancastrian cause was doomed. The Yorkists proclaimed Richard's son King Edward IV and won the decisive battle of Towton. The Lancastrian dynasty was eliminated in 1471, when Henry VI's teenage heir was stabbed to death after the Battle of Tewkesbury and Henry VI himself was murdered in the Tower.

The 1480s brought the murder of the princes in the Tower and the overthrow of the House of York when Richard III was unhorsed at Bosworth Field and the Tudor dynasty founded. Thus, in the second half of the fifteenth century, deciding who was to be king of England took priority over any English pretensions to the throne of France.

Meanwhile in France the real French king, now clearly recognised as such, celebrated the recovery of his kingdom and consolidated his hold on it. Charles VII lost no opportunity to curb the power of the Duke of Burgundy. Philip the Good must have wondered whether his decision to change sides in 1435 had in fact served his own best interests.

Charles VII also, belatedly, paid his debt to Joan of Arc. He ordered a retrial of her case. After a slow start this led to a reversal of the original verdict of heresy. Joan's sentence was annulled (it was only in the early twentieth century that Joan was declared a saint). The rehabilitation of Joan of Arc reinforced the legitimacy of Charles VII's coronation, which in turn strengthened the perception of his right to govern all the territory he had reconquered from the English.

The French monarchy's other fundamental task was to repair, as fast as was practical, the damage the country had suffered during so many decades of warfare and brigandage. This situation was more severe in some areas than in others but in most of northern and central France, especially Normandy, the Loire and the region around Paris, life in the countryside remained scarred for many years. Thomas Basin, a French chronicler, has left this account from around 1461:

> From the Loire to the Seine, and from there to the Somme, nearly all the fields were left for a long time, for many years, not merely untended but without people capable of cultivating them, except for rare patches of soil,

for the peasants had been killed or put to flight. . . . We ourselves have seen the vast plains of Champagne, Beauce, Brie, Gâtinais, Chartres, Dreux, Maine and Perche, Vexin, both French and Norman, Beauvais, Caux, from the Seine as far as Amiens and Abbeville, Senlis, Soissonnais, Valois, as far as Laon and, beyond, as far as Hainault, absolutely deserted, uncultivated, abandoned, devoid of all inhabitants, overgrown with brushwood. . . . All one could cultivate then in those regions was around and inside towns, strongholds or castles, close enough for the look-out man from his tower or post to be able to spot the brigands as they came up to attack. Then, ringing the bell or sounding the trumpet, or by some other means, he would signal all those working in the fields or vineyards to fall back within the walls. . . . It is not unusual now for oxen and workhorses, at the sound of the signal from the guard . . . to stampede like creatures possessed to regain the refuge where they feel safe.

Writing a few years later the Englishman John Fortescue said of the French peasants: 'They live in the most extreme poverty and misery, and yet they dwell in one of the most fertile realms of the world.'

Charles VII died in 1461, so much of the task of reconstruction, and of consolidating French royal power, was handed on to his son Louis XI. In 1475 Louis had to face a further English invasion. During a period when tenure of the English throne was relatively settled, Edward IV started scheming with Burgundy against France. However, when Edward and an English army actually landed at Calais, Burgundian support failed to materialize. Left on his own to face the French army, Edward IV decided to negotiate – and the wily French king essentially bribed him to go home again. Under the Treaty of Picquigny, Edward IV settled for a down payment of 75,000 crowns, an annual pension of 60,000 crowns and a banquet. Louis XI boasted: 'I have chased the English out of France more easily than my father ever did, for my father drove them out by force of arms, whereas I have driven them out with venison pies and good wine.'

At Picquigny (near Amiens) the two kings also agreed to a seven-year truce and a commitment to settle any differences between their two kingdoms by arbitration. Edward's IV's eldest daughter would marry the Dauphin, while Louis XI would pay a further sum to purchase the freedom of Henry VI's French widow, Margaret of Anjou.

Some historians have argued that the 1475 Treaty of Picquigny, rather than the 1453 Battle of Castillon, should be regarded as the true end of the Anglo-French conflict. But there was no tidy end. The Tudor kings Henry VII and Henry VIII both invaded France, to little effect, and it was the Tudor Queen Mary who finally lost Calais to the French in 1558.

Even then, English monarchs continued to style themselves kings or queens of France until 1802 when, following the French Revolution and during the Napoleonic wars, there was no longer a French king of France – only the exiled Louis XVIII whom the English subsequently helped to restore.

Assessment

Reviewing the whole saga, what are we to make of the Hundred Years War? However strong the plot, it should not be seen simply as a royal soap opera. Beneath it lay economic rivalries in the cloth and wine trades – and the breakdown of economic organization and prosperity in the wake of the Black Death. Importantly, the conflict reflected power struggles on both sides of the English Channel between kings and the most powerful magnates in their respective kingdoms. Indeed the warfare in France, particularly in the first half of the fifteenth century, can in many respects be viewed as a civil war in which the English intervened.

The Hundred Years War can also be seen as the period during which France and England became separate nations. France expelled the English from Normandy and Aquitaine and, albeit after the end of the war, integrated the separate duchies of Burgundy and Brittany into the French kingdom. Joan of Arc touched a chord of collective hostility to the English invaders, related to some common feeling of being French. The country of France, with a more stable set of borders and a clearer sense of identity, had taken shape.

By being expelled, and then tacitly abandoning any serious attempt to reconquer Normandy and Aquitaine, the English came to terms with their own borders as an island. During the course of the Hundred Years War, the English court ceased to speak French as its main language. Only when the Wars of the Roses were over, in Tudor times, did England achieve a relatively settled identity as a nation – but the Hundred Years War, and in particular the final defeat, played an important role in forging it.

During the war feudal power slowly gave way to royal power and feudal armies were supplemented, and increasingly replaced, by professional armies. Archery began to be eclipsed by artillery. The cost of keeping an effective professional army in the field, not to mention establishing naval supremacy, was significant, and had an influence on patterns of taxation, which in turn affected relations between monarchs and parliaments.

Perhaps the other observation to make is that this was a period of human suffering. Barbara Tuchman's book, *A Distant Mirror*, noting parallels between the 'calamitous' fourteenth century and the first half of the twentieth century, terms it 'a violent, tormented, bewildered, suffering and disintegrating age'.

How did such French peasants as survived the Black Death, the periodic famines, the destructive military raids and the marauding brigands feel about the quality of their lives, relative to what they knew of their parents' and grandparents' experience? What did the Black Prince and the Duke of Bedford think about their own lifetime achievements as they lay dying? How did the Duke of Suffolk's family feel about the way he was murdered for serving his country in high office? When they invaded France, did Edward III and Henry V have any real insight into the likely implications of their actions and the intractable problems they were to bequeath to their successors?

The legends passed down from the chroniclers, interpreted patriotically over the centuries, have created an aura of chivalry and heroic military valour around the Hundred Years War. For visitors to the sites today, reliving the battles and dramatic reversals of royal fortunes of the fourteenth and fifteenth centuries, some reflection on the suffering, destruction and waste of that era should also form part of our perspective.

Chronology

1327	Edward III becomes king of England
1328	Death of Charles IV of France; Philip VI becomes king of France
1337	Edward III claims to be king of France; start of the war
1340	Flanders supports Edward III, who wins the Battle of Sluys
1346	Edward III invades Normandy and wins the Battle of Crécy
1347	Edward III finally captures Calais after a long siege
1347-50	Black Death hits France and then England
1350	Death of Philip VI; John the Good becomes king of France
1355	The Black Prince leads a raid across southern France
1356	The Black Prince captures John the Good in the Battle of Poitiers
1359–60	Edward III's invasion of France ends on 'Black Monday'
1360	The Treaty of Brétigny represents a major English victory
1364	Death of John the Good; Charles V becomes king of France
1367	The Black Prince wins a battle in Spain that later proves very costly
1369	Charles V declares Aquitaine confiscated and restarts the war
1369–74	Charles V and Bertrand du Guesclin overturn England's conquests
1376	Death of the Black Prince leaves his young son heir to the throne
1377	Death of Edward III: Richard II becomes king of England
1380	Death of Charles V; Charles VI becomes king of France
1386	French invasion of England is aborted
1389	Richard II and Charles VI conclude Truce of Leulinghen
1392	Charles VI has a spell of madness and remains intermittently mad

204

1396	Richard II marries Charles VI's daughter: long-term truce agreed
1399	Richard II is deposed by his rival who becomes King Henry IV
1407	Murder of the Duke of Orléans sparks civil war in France
1413	Death of Henry IV; Henry V becomes king of England
1415	Henry V invades France and wins the Battle of Agincourt
1417–19	Henry V conquers Normandy
1419	Murder of the Duke of Burgundy; his heir allies with Henry V
1420	Treaty of Troyes; Henry V becomes Charles VI's son-in-law and heir
1422	Death of Henry V; Henry VI becomes king of England; death of Charles VI; is Henry VI of England now also king of France?
1424	Duke of Bedford's victory at Verneuil boosts 'dual monarchy'
1429	Joan of Arc meets the Dauphin and raises the English siege of Orléans; the Dauphin is crowned King Charles VII of France at Reims
1431	Following her capture and trial, Joan of Arc is burnt at the stake; Henry VI of England is crowned 'Henri II' of France in Paris
1435	The Duke of Burgundy switches allegiance from England to France
1436	Charles VII recaptures Paris
1444	Truce of Tours; Henry VI marries Margaret of Anjou
1449–50	Charles VII reconquers Normandy
1451–53	Charles VII conquers Aquitaine; war ends with the Battle of Castillon

List of Principal Characters

In view of its brevity, the account of the Hundred Years War in this book omits many figures – among them, military commanders, barons, courtiers and popes – who feature in the history books. Even so, a large number of characters are introduced in this narrative and listed below, for reference, are the principal ones.

Alençon, Duke of	French military commander who fought with Joan of Arc
Armagnac, Bernard, Count of	Leader of the faction of followers of Louis, Duke of Orléans after the latter's murder in 1407
Armagnac, John, Count of	French military commander faced with the Black Prince's raid of 1355
Balliol, Edward	King of Scotland, son of John Balliol. Gained crown by deposing David II in 1332
Beaufort, Cardinal	Henry, Bishop of Winchester. Legitimized son of John of Gaunt. Minister under Henry VI and leader of the 'peace faction' in the 1430s
Bedford, John, Duke of	Brother of Henry V and uncle of Henry VI, Regent in France for Henry VI

Berry, John, Duke of

Son of John the Good, brother of Charles V and uncle of Charles VI. Patron of the arts

Blois, Charles and Jeanne of

Count and Countess of Blois. Claimants to the duchy of Brittany after 1341

Buch, Captal (Lord) of

Jean de Grailly. Gascon military commander who fought under the Black Prince

Buchan, Earl of

Scots military commander serving the Dauphin. Fought against the English. Killed in battle 1424

Bureau, Jean

Charles VII's artillery expert, aided by his brother, Gaspard

Burgundy, John, Duke of

John the Fearless. Son of Philip the Bold and father of Philip the Good

Burgundy, Philip, Duke of

Philip the Bold. Son of John the Good, brother of Charles V and uncle of Charles VI. Father of John the Fearless

Burgundy, Philip, Duke of

Philip the Good. Son of John the Fearless and ally of Henry V and the Duke of Bedford. Changed sides in 1435

Cade, Jack

Leader of rebellion in England in 1450

Catherine of France

Daughter of Charles VI and Queen of England. Married Henry V

Cauchon, Pierre

Bishop of Beauvais. Oversaw trial of Joan of Arc

Chandos, Sir John	Military commander under Edward III and the Black Prince
Charles IV	King of France, reigned 1322–28. Brother of Isabella of France
Charles V	King of France, reigned 1364–80. Previously, the Dauphin. Known as Charles the Wise
Charles VI	King of France, reigned 1380–1422. Went mad
Charles VII	Called the Dauphin until his coronation in 1429. King of France, reigned 1422–61
Charles the Bad	King of Navarre. French royal family. Enemy or fickle ally of John the Good and Charles V
Clarence, Thomas, Duke of	Brother of Henry V. Killed in battle in 1421
Coeur, Jacques	Merchant and financier who served Charles VII
Dagworth, Sir Thomas	Edward III's military commander in Brittany
David II	Son of Robert the Bruce, became boy king of Scotland in 1329. Deposed in 1332, then in temporary exile in France
Dunois, John, Count of	The Bastard of Orléans. Half-brother of Charles of Orléans. French military commander under the Dauphin/Charles VII
Edward II	King of England, reigned 1307–27. Father of Edward III
Edward III	King of England, reigned 1327–77. Claimed also to be King of France

Edward, the Black Prince	Eldest son of Edward III, died 1376
Eleanor of Aquitaine	Queen of France, then Queen of England. Married Henry II of England (reigned 1154–89)
Fastolf, Sir John	Military commander under Henry V and Henry VI
Gaunt, John of	Son of Edward III. Became Duke of Lancaster by marriage. Brother of the Black Prince. Uncle of Richard II and father of Henry IV
Gloucester, Thomas, Duke of	Thomas of Woodstock. Youngest son of Edward III and uncle of Richard II. Leader of a group of barons critical of Richard II
Gloucester, Humphrey, Duke of	Brother of Henry V and uncle of Henry VI. Led the 'war faction' in the 1430s and 1440s
Guesclin, Bertrand du	Military commander under Charles V of France. Became Constable of France and a French hero
Harcourt, Godfrey of	Normandy noble who supported Edward III. Subsequently changed sides more than once
Henry IV	Henry Bolingbroke, son of John of Gaunt. Earl of Derby and Duke of Lancaster. King of England, reigned 1399–1413
Henry V	King of England, reigned 1413–22. Victor of Agincourt. Son-in-law of Charles VI
Henry VI	King of England, reigned 1422–61. Also crowned 'Henri II' of France

Isabeau of Bavaria	Queen of France. Married Charles VI (reigned 1380–1422). Mother of the Dauphin Charles, who ultimately became Charles VII
Isabella of France	Daughter of Philip IV. Queen of England. Married Edward II and, with her lover, Roger Mortimer, forced his abdication
Isabella of France	Daughter of Charles VI. Briefly Queen of England. Married Richard II in 1396
Joan of Arc	Heroine of the siege of Orléans. Secured the coronation of Charles VII. Burned as a heretic by the English in 1431. Now a saint
John the Good	King John II of France, reigned 1350–64
Kyriel, Sir Thomas	English military commander defeated in Normandy in 1450
Lancaster, Henry, Earl and later Duke of	Edward III's military commander in France
Lancaster, other Dukes of	see John of Gaunt and Henry IV
Luxembourg, Jean de	Burgundian count. Captured Joan of Arc
Luxembourg, John of	King of Bohemia. Blind. Killed at Crécy
Marcel, Etienne	Leader of Paris merchants' revolt of 1357–58
Margaret of Anjou	French princess and Queen of England. Married Henry VI

Montfort, John of	Claimant to the duchy of Brittany after 1341. Supported by Edward III. Died 1345
Montfort, John of	Son of the above John. Became Duke John IV of Brittany. Switched allegiance more than once
Orléans, Bastard of	see Dunois, John, Count of
Orléans, Charles, Duke of	Son of Louis. Captured at Agincourt in 1415 and imprisoned in England until 1440
Orléans, Louis, Duke of	Brother of Charles VI. Murdered in 1407
Pedro the Cruel	King of Castile. Supported by the Black Prince
Philip VI	First Valois King of France, reigned 1328–50
Philippa of Hainault	Daughter of the Count of Hainault, Queen of England. Married Edward III
Richard II	Richard of Bordeaux, son of the Black Prince. King of England, reigned 1377–99. Deposed
Richemont, Arthur de	Constable of France under Charles VII
Rolin, Nicolas	Chancellor to Philip the Good, Duke of Burgundy and adviser on interpretation of the Treaty of Troyes
Salisbury, Earl of	William Montagu. Military commander under the Black Prince
Salisbury, Earl of	Thomas Montagu. Military commander under Henry V and Henry VI. Killed at Orléans 1428

Somerset, Edmund, Duke of	English military commander in France under Henry VI. Later involved in Wars of the Roses
Sorel, Agnès	Charles VII's mistress
Suffolk, Earl and later Duke of	William de la Pole. Minister under Henry VI
Surienne, François de	Aragonese mercenary who led English attack on Fougères in 1449
Talbot, John	Earl of Shrewsbury. Military commander under Henry V and Henry VI
Trastamara, Henry of	Pedro the Cruel's rival for the throne of Castile
Tyler, Wat	Leader of Peasants' Revolt in England of 1381
Vienne, Jean de	Defender of Calais in 1346–47 and French admiral
Warwick, Earl of	Thomas de Beauchamp. Military commander under Edward III and the Black Prince
Warwick, Earl of	Thomas Beauchamp, allied with Thomas, Duke of Gloucester as critic of Richard II
Warwick, Earl of	Richard Beauchamp. Military commander under Henry V and Henry VI
York, Richard, Duke of	English military commander in France under Henry VI. Great-grandson of Edward III and led the Yorkists against the Lancastrians in the Wars of the Roses. Father of Edward IV

Notes

Introduction

Page 1: 'Hundred Years War' a term dating from the nineteenth century. Anne Curry. *The Hundred Years War* (Macmillan, Basingstoke, 1993) p. 24.

Notes to Chapter 1

Page 5: description of Edward III. Desmond Seward. *The Hundred Years War* (Constable, London, 1978) p. 29; W.M. Ormrod. *The Reign of Edward III* (Yale, New Haven and London, 1990) p. 44.

Page 5: scene in marketplace in Ghent. Jonathan Sumption. *The Hundred Years War*. Vol. 1, *Trial by Battle* (Faber, London, 1990. Paperback version University of Pennsylvania Press, 1999) p. 302; Seward, op.cit., p. 39; May McKisack. *The Fourteenth Century* (Oxford University Press, Oxford, 1959) p. 128.

Pages 8–9: 'liege homage'. Robin Neillands. *The Hundred Years War* (Guild, London, 1990) p. 18; Sumption, op.cit., p. 73.

Page 9: 'too much given to sodomy'. The chronicler of the Abbey of Meaux quoted by Caroline Bingham. *Edward II* (Weidenfeld & Nicholson, London, 1973) p. 54. Caroline Bingham also adds that 'of the precise nature of (Edward II's) relations with Gaveston there is no evidence at all'.

Page 10: homage to successive French kings. Edouard Perroy. *The Hundred Years War* (Eyre & Spottiswoode, London, 1962) p. 64; Sumption, op.cit., p. 86.

Page 10: Saint-Sardos. Sumption, op.cit., p. 91 ff.; Perroy, op.cit., p. 65.

Page 12: murder of Edward II. Bingham, op.cit., p. 197.

Page 13: 'the son of a king and would not do homage to the son of a count', quoted by Sumption, op.cit., p. 109.

Page 15: homage ceremony at Amiens. Perroy, op.cit., p. 82; Sumption, op.cit., p. 110–11; Neillands, op.cit., p. 37.

Page 15: 'fair son, have pity on gentle Mortimer', quoted by Seward, op.cit., p. 20, and by Sumption, op.cit., p. 115.

Page 16: Amiens feature quotation: Barbara Tuchman. *A Distant Mirror* (Macmillan, London, 1979, and Papermac, 1995) p. 12.

Page 18: 'endure with good humour and fair words. . . .' quoted in Perroy, op.cit., p. 84.

Page 18: journey to Pont-Sainte-Maxence in disguise. Sumption, op.cit., p. 117; McKisack, op.cit., p. 112.

Page 19: Edward III wept over English humiliation by Scots. Seward, op.cit., p. 27.

Pages 19–20: relationship between Scotland and the start of the Hundred Years War. Anne Curry, op.cit., p. 137–45.

Page 20: exiled Scottish court at Château-Gaillard. Sumption, op.cit., p. 135–7. Feature on Château-Gaillard also draws on Achille Deville. *Histoire du Château-Gaillard* (originally published in 1829, Editions Page de Garde) and on *La France Médiévale* (Guides Gallimard, Paris, 1998) p. 243–5.

Page 20: French warships. Sumption, op.cit., p. 164 ff.

Page 21: 'mortal enemy'. Sumption, op.cit., p. 184.

Page 21: 'we give you notice that. . . .' Sumption, op.cit., p. 232.

Page 24: Froissart quoted by Neillands, op.cit., p. 79–80.

Page 24: Scots from Château-Gaillard. Sumption, op.cit., p. 273.

Page 24: pawned the crown. Seward, op.cit., p. 37.

Page 25: Jean Le Bel quotation. Peter E. Thompson (Ed.) *Contemporary Chronicles of the Hundred Years War* (The Folio Society, London, 1966) p. 54.

Page 26: terms of Parliament's subsidy. Neillands, op.cit., p. 82; Sumption, op.cit., p. 306.

Notes to Chapter 2

Page 27: 'The King of England and his fleet are coming down on us. . .', quoted in Seward, op.cit., p. 44.

Pages 27–28: Battle of Sluys. Seward, op.cit., p. 42–6; Neillands, op.cit., p. 83–4; Sumption op.cit. p. 324–7; Norman Davies. *The Isles – A History* (Macmillan, London, 1999) p. 415.

Page 28: fish and French blood. Tuchman, op.cit., p. 71.

Page 28: Fool's riddle. Neillands, op.cit., p. 84; Tuchman, op.cit., p. 71.

Pages 28–9: Brittany. Sumption, op.cit., p. 385–454; Perroy, op.cit., p. 115; Neillands, op.cit., 87–91; Seward, op.cit., p. 49.

Pages 29–30: preparations for invasion. Sumption, op.cit., p. 489–99; Seward, op.cit., p. 51; Tuchman, op.cit., p. 81–82.

Page 31: Godfrey of Harcourt quotation from Froissart's Chronicles, quoted by McKisack, op.cit., p. 133.

Page 31–4: Jean le Bel quotation from Thompson, op.cit., p. 60–1.

Page 35: sack of Caen. Seward, op.cit., p. 59; Neillands, op.cit., p. 95; Sumption, op.cit., p. 507–11.

Page 35: the Seine. Neillands, op.cit., p. 96; Sumption, op.cit., p. 514–8.

Page 39–40: the Somme. Neillands, op.cit., p. 97; Sumption, op.cit., p. 521–4; Seward, op.cit., p. 60.

Page 41: longbow, Bryan Bevan. *Edward III* (Rubicon, London, 1992) p. 68; Sumption, op.cit., p. 532.

Page 41: cannon. Bevan, op.cit., p. 74–75; Neillands, op.cit., p. 102; Sumption, op.cit., p. 527.

Page 41: 'gave orders. . .', Jean le Bel quotations from Thompson, op.cit., p. 72.

Page 41: size of French army. Neillands, op.cit., p. 100; Seward, op. cit. p. 63.

Page 44: 'These brave knights. . .', Jean le Bel quotation from Thompson, op.cit., p. 69–70.

Pages 44–7: Battle of Crécy. Alan Lloyd. *The Hundred Years War* (Book Club Associates, London, 1977) p. 55–9; Bevan, op.cit., p. 73–6; Neillands, op.cit., p. 99–104; Seward, op.cit., p. 63–8; Sumption, op.cit., p. 525–32.

Page 47: Godfrey of Harcourt. Sumption, op.cit., p. 533–4.

Page 48: Calais feature: names of the six burghers. Bevan, op.cit., p. 78.

Page 50: Jean le Bel quotation from Thompson, op.cit., p. 74.

Page 50: assault on Calais. Sumption, op.cit., p. 558.

Page 51: troop numbers. Sumption, op.cit., p. 578.

Page 51: Jean de Vienne letter including quotation. Sumption, op.cit., p. 577.

Page 51: expulsion of the 500. Neillands, op.cit., p. 105; Seward, op.cit., p. 69; Sumption, op.cit., p. 577.

Page 52: 'Tell him from me. . .', Jean le Bel quotation from Thompson, op.cit., p. 78.

Page 52–3: Jean le Bel quotations, ibid. pp. 80 and 82.

Page 53: Estates spokesman quoted by Neillands, op.cit., p. 110.

Notes to Chapter 3

Page 54: Black Prince's name. Neillands, op.cit., p. 122.

Page 54: News of Sluys. Richard Barber. *Edward, Prince of Wales and Aquitaine* (Boydell Press, Woodbridge, 1978) p. 34.

Page 54: Order of the Garter. Barber, op.cit., p. 83–92; Neillands, op.cit., p. 112–3; Seward, op.cit., p. 72.

Page 55–6: The Black Death. Neillands, op.cit., p. 110–12; Tuchman, op.cit., p. 92–125; Jonathan Sumption. *The Hundred Years War*. Vol. II *Trial by Fire* (Faber, London, 1999) p. 6–10.

Page 56: Character of John the Good. Seward, op.cit., p. 78; Sumption, op.cit., p. 68; Neillands, op.cit., p. 116.

Page 56: Combat of the Thirty. Tuchman, op.cit., p. 131; Sumption, op.cit., p. 33–4; Neillands, op.cit., p. 118; Seward, op.cit., p. 79.

Page 58: Murder of Charles of Spain. Tuchman, op.cit., p. 133; Sumption, op.cit., p. 124–5.

Page 58: Treaty of Guines. Neillands, op.cit., p. 120; Sumption, op.cit., p. 135–6.

Pages 59–63: The Black Prince's raid. Seward, op.cit., p. 84–5; Barber, op.cit., p. 116–28; Sumption, op.cit., p. 175–87.

Page 59: 'Harrying and wasting the country...' quoted in Tuchman, op.cit., p. 138.

Page 68: Charles and Bad's arrest, 'Foul traitor, you deserve to die'. Sumption, op.cit., p. 205–6.

Pages 68–70: Black Prince's 1356 march. Barber, op.cit., 132–6; Sumption, op.cit., 226–33.

Page 70: Froissart quotation from Thompson, op.cit., p. 98.

Page 71: 'Fair lords, we are but few...' ibid., p. 110.

Pages 71–5: Battle of Poitiers. Barber, op.cit., 138–48; Sumption, op.cit., p. 235–49; Tuchman, op.cit., p. 145–54; Neillands, op.cit., p. 126–32; Seward, op.cit., p. 87–94; Lloyd, op.cit., p. 87–100.

Page 75: Froissart quotation from Thompson, op.cit., p. 115.

Page 75: 'You lie, you miserable coward...' quoted in Seward, op.cit., p. 90, and Tuchman, op.cit., p. 150.

Page 75: 'Come, John...' Froissart from Thompson, op.cit., p. 113.

Pages 76–7: Froissart's account of John the Good's surrender, ibid., p. 118 and p. 120.

Page 77: Froissart quotation 'Throughout the evening...' ibid., p. 123.

Page 77: 'Well, I see we must call you...' quoted in Neillands, op.cit., p. 132.

Page 77: triumphal entry into London. Barber, op.cit., p. 152; Sumption, op.cit., p. 290; Tuchman, op.cit., p. 168; Seward, op.cit., p. 94–5.

Page 79: Froissart quotation from Penguin edition selected, translated and edited by Geoffrey Brereton (Penguin, London, 1968) p. 151 and p. 152.

Pages 80–1: 1359 invasion and 1360 treaty. Barber, op.cit., p. 159–69; Tuchman, op.cit., p. 185–90; Sumption, op.cit., p. 424–503; Seward, op.cit., p. 97–101; Neillands, op.cit., p. 157–60.

Page 80: Froissart quotation from Brereton, op.cit., p. 164–5.

Page 81: 3,000 butts of wine. Seward, op.cit., p. 98.

Notes to Chapter 4

Page 85: Charles V's character. Perroy, op.cit., p. 146; Sumption, op.cit., p. 511; Seward, op.cit., p. 103–4.

Pages 85–6: Du Guesclin. Yves Jacob. *Bertrand du Guesclin* (Tallandier, Paris, 1992) p. 47–8 in 1999 edition; M. Coryn. *Black Mastiff* (Arthur Barker, London, 1933) p. 27–52; Sumption, op.cit., p. 506.

Page 88: Charles V's ambitions. Sumption, op.cit., p. 512.

Pages 89–90: Free Companies. Sumption, op.cit., p. 38–44, 360–1, 410–11; Seward, op.cit., p. 104–6, 118; Neillands, op.cit., p. 162; Perroy, op.cit., p. 155.

Page 91: Size of the Black Prince's army. Sumption, op.cit., p. 547.

Page 91: Pedro's debt. Sumption, op.cit., p. 557.

Page 92: Black Prince's financial position. Sumption, op.cit., p. 568–69, Perroy, op.cit., p. 159; Neillands, op.cit., p. 164; Seward, op.cit., p. 208–9; Barber, op.cit., p. 109.

Page 92: Charles V's preparations for war. Perroy, op.cit., p. 163; Seward, op.cit., p. 109.

Page 93: 'In his capacity as the sovereign lord. . .' quoted in Sumption, op.cit., p. 574.

Page 93: Further appeals. Neillands, op.cit., p. 167.

Page 93: 'We will willingly go to Paris. . .' quoted in Barber, op.cit., p. 219; Neillands, op.cit., p. 167.

Page 93: Edward III's resumption of title of king of France. Sumption, op.cit., p. 585.

Page 94: Renewal of the war, 1369–70. Perroy, op.cit., p. 164.

Pages 94–5: Froissart quotation from Brereton edition, op.cit., p. 177–8.

Page 95: Capture of the Captal of Buch. Jacob, op.cit., p. 223–4.

Page 95: 'God and St George help us.' quoted in Seward, op.cit., p. 114.

Pages 95–8: John of Gaunt's 1373 expedition. Perroy, op.cit., p. 164; Seward, op.cit., p. 114.

Page 98: Froissart quotation from Brereton edition, op.cit., p. 193.

Page 99: Succession through the female line ruled out. Report on British Library document, *Times*, London, 18 July 1997.

Page 101: Death of Du Guesclin. Coryn, op.cit., p. 282ff.

Page 101: Charles V's offer of daughter in marriage. Perroy, op.cit., p. 173.

Page 101: 'The first King of England since the Norman Conquest...' John Julius Norwich. *Shakespeare's Kings* (Viking, London, 1999) p. 72.

Page 104: 'You are the greatest King living...' quoted in Tuchman, op.cit., p. 424.

Page 105: Froissart quotations from Thompson, op.cit., p. 185.

Page 105: Pre-fabricated fortress. Seward, op.cit., p. 134; Tuchman, op.cit., p. 426.

Pages 105–6: 'Dear brother...' and 'Even supposing...' Froissart quotations from Thompson op.cit. p. 195–96.

Page 106: Richard II and Duke of Gloucester. Norwich, op.cit., p. 82; Seward, op.cit., p. 136.

Page 107: Charles VI's madness. Tuchman, op.cit., p. 498; Perroy, op.cit., p. 194.

Page 107: Richard II's concession on homage. Perroy, op.cit., p. 197.

Page 108: Richard II's request for canonisation of Edward II. Norwich, op.cit., p. 96–97, Perroy, op.cit., p. 200.

Notes to Chapter 5

Page 110: madness of Charles VI. Seward, op.cit., p. 143; Neillands, op.cit., p. 186–87.

Page 111: quotation of Louis, Duke of Orléans. From the chronicle of Enguerrand de Monstrelet, quoted in Bryan Bevan. *Henry IV* (Rubicon Press, London, 1994) p. 87.

Page 113: Dijon feature: history of the Jacquemart clock. Michelin Tourist Guide to Burgundy and Jura, 1995, p. 148.

Page 114: harsh, crafty and a dangerous enemy. Perroy, op.cit., p. 226.

Page 114: the wooden club and the carpenter's plane. Seward, op.cit., p. 148.

Page 114: Enguerrand de Monstrelet quotation from Thompson, op.cit., p. 258–9.

Page 114: 'Know you that by my orders was the Duke of Orléans killed', quoted by Neillands, op.cit., p. 187.

Page 115: burning of John Badby. Seward, op.cit., p. 154.

Page 116: 'With regard to those things you claim, you have no right, . . .', quoted by Neillands, op.cit., p. 201.

Page 116: Dick Whittington. Seward, op.cit., p. 156. Neillands, op.cit., p. 202.

Page 116: military pay. Neillands, op.cit., p. 203.

Page 117: *Trinity Royal*, 500 tons and crew of 300. Alan Lloyd, op.cit., p. 135.

Page 117: Le Havre did not then exist. Lloyd, op.cit., p. 136.

Page 117: Sir John Fastolf the first ashore. Neillands, op.cit., p. 205.

Pages 117–8: siege of Harfleur. Richard Holmes. *War Walks – From Agincourt to Normandy* (BBC Books, London, 1996) p. 26.

Page 118: challenge of single combat to Dauphin. Holmes, op.cit., p. 27; Neillands, op.cit., p. 209.

Page 119: Battle of Agincourt – size of armies, Henry's speech, and location. Christopher Hibbert. *Agincourt* (Windrush Press, Moreton-in-Marsh, 1996 edition) p. 76–79.

Page 119: Enguerrand de Monstrelet quotation, Thompson, op.cit., p. 278

Pages 119–123: course of the battle of Agincourt. Hibbert, op.cit., p. 85–92; Neillands, op.cit., p. 211–221; Seward, op.cit., p. 162–9; Lloyd, op.cit., p. 147–57; Holmes, op.cit., p. 28–49.

Page 123: death of Duke of York. Sir Charles Oman. *The Art of War in the Middle Ages Volume II* (Greenhill Books, London, 1998) p. 386 (originally published in its two volume version in 1924).

Page 124: 'It is not we but God Almighty. . .' Quoted by Enguerrand de Monstrelet, Thompson, op.cit., p. 280–81.

Page 124: 'Welcome, Henry the Fifte, Kynge of England and of Fraunce'. Quoted by Peter Earle. *The Life and Times of Henry V* (Weidenfeld & Nicholson, London, 1972) p. 145.

Page 124: change from raids to policy of conquest. Christopher Allmand. *The Hundred Years War* (Cambridge University Press, Cambridge, 1989) p. 29.

Page 124: goose feathers for arrow-making. Seward, op.cit., p. 71.

Page 125: at least one French historian. Joseph Calmette. *The Golden Age of Burgundy* (Weidenfeld & Nicholson, London, 1962, translated from French edition of 1949) p. 117–8.

Page 125: French monk. Earle, op.cit., p. 158.

Pages 126–7: siege of Rouen, Earle, op.cit., p. 166–70; Neillands, op.cit., p. 227; Seward, op.cit., p. 175–7.

Page 127: John Page quotation. Seward, op.cit., p. 177.

Page 127: Queen Isabeau's lover. Earle, op.cit., p. 183.

Page 127: 'Queen of France, having on behalf of our Lord the King government and administration of the kingdom'. Calmette, op.cit., p. 119.

Page 132: Charles VI thanks the Duke of Burgundy for his kindness to the Queen. Calmette, op.cit., p. 122.

Page 132: 'This is the hole through which the English entered France'. Seward, op.cit., p. 180; Neillands, op.cit., p. 229.

Page 133: Treaty of Troyes. Quoted by Enguerrand de Monstrelet, Thompson, op.cit., p. 286–8.

Page 134: two royal courts. Enguerrand de Monstrelet, Thompson, op.cit., p. 288–9.

Notes to Chapter 6

Page 142: battle of Baugé. Neillands, op.cit., p. 233–4; Seward, op.cit., p. 185–6.

Page 143: Henry V quotations from Enguerrand de Monstrelet's chronicle, Thompson, op.cit., p. 290–91.

Page 143: Henry V's funeral procession. Earle, op.cit., p. 214.

Page 144: Battle of Verneuil. Seward, op.cit., p. 198–201; Neillands, op.cit., p. 241.

Page 145: Jean de Wavrin quotation. Seward op.cit., p. 200.

Page 145: Fastolf's ransom for the Duke of Alençon. Seward, op.cit., p. 243.

Page 145: Bedford quotation. Seward, op.cit., p. 201.

Page 145–6: Jacqueline of Hainault. Perroy, op.cit., p. 270–2; Seward, op.cit., p. 202; Neillands, op.cit., p. 248–49.

Page 146: 'Joyeux Repos' Seward, op.cit., p. 221.

Page 147: death of Salisbury. Neillands, op.cit., p. 255; Seward, op.cit., p. 210.

Page 152: 'very angry to have beaten the bushes'. Quoted in Edward Lucie-Smith. *Joan of Arc* (Allen Lane, London, 1976) p. 93.

Page 152: Burgundian attacks on Domrémy. Lucie-Smith, op.cit., p. 21 and 25.

Page 152: Quotation from documentation of Joan of Arc's trial. W.P. Barrett (trans.) *The Trial of Jeanne d'Arc* (Routledge, London, 1931) p. 63–4.

Pages 153–8: Joan of Arc's letter. Quoted in Lucie-Smith, op.cit., p. 78–9.

Page 158: Joan's entry into Orléans. Lucie-Smith, op.cit., p. 99–102.

Page 158–9: fighting in Orléans. Lucie-Smith, op.cit., p. 103–121; Neillands, op.cit., p. 259–60; Seward, op.cit., p. 216; Kelly Devries. *Joan of Arc, A Military Leader* (Sutton, Stroud, 1999) p. 54–96.

Page 159: prisoners at Jargeau massacred. Lucie-Smith, op.cit., p. 133.

Page 159: Enguerrand de Monstrelet quotation. Thompson, op.cit., p. 305–6.

Page 160: 'And at the hour when the king...' Quoted in Lucie-Smith, op.cit., p. 161.

Page 160: 'Gentle King...' From the chronicle of Jean Chartier, quoted by Marina Warner. *Joan of Arc* (Vintage, London, 1981) p. 72.

Page 161: 'It is true that the King...' Quoted by Marina Warner, op.cit., p. 73.

Page 161: 'a disorderly and disgraced woman'. Quoted by Seward, op.cit., p. 219.

Pages 161–4: Enguerrand de Monstrelet quotation. Thompson, op.cit., p. 312.

Page 164: 'I know well...' Quoted in Lucie-Smith op.cit., p. 212.

Page 164: 'Why should she speak English? ...' Barrett, op.cit., p. 187.

Page 165: 'This woman is apostate ...' ibid., p. 292; 'I Jeanne, ...' ibid., p. 313.

Page 165: '... since you are fallen again...' ibid, p. 329.

Page 166: Enguerrand de Monstrelet quotation. Thompson, op.cit., p. 316.

Notes to Chapter 7

Page 168: reinterpretation of Treaty of Troyes. Neillands, op.cit., p. 268; Jocelyn Gledhill Dickinson. *The Congress of Arras* (Clarendon Press, Oxford, 1955) p. 66–77.

Page 168–9: the Congress of Arras. Neillands, op.cit., p. 268–70; Seward, op.cit., p. 230–3; Perroy, op.cit., p. 291–5; Dickinson, op.cit., p. 118–9.

Page 169: 'abandoned me in my boyhood...' quoted by Neillands, op.cit., p. 270.

Page 169: lynching of Burgundian merchants, Seward, op.cit., p. 234.

Page 172: 'He showed them a general amnesty...' Enguerrand de Monstrelet's chronicle, Thompson, op.cit., p. 321.

Page 173: character of Henry VI. Seward, op.cit., p. 234–35; Norwich, op.cit., p. 227.

Page 174: Eleanor of Cobham. Norwich, op.cit., p. 229; Neillands, op.cit., p. 278.

Page 175: Suffolk's background. Seward, op.cit., p. 244; Norwich, op.cit., p. 229.

Pages 175–8: Suffolk's embassy and the king's marriage. Norwich, op.cit., p. 230–1; R.A. Griffiths. *The Reign of King Henry VI* (Sutton, Stroud, 1981) p. 484–7 (1998 edition); Bertram Wolffe. *Henry VI* (Eyre Methuen, London, 1981) p. 176.

Page 178: Henry VI's letter about Maine. Wolffe, op.cit., p. 185.

Page 178: 'our most dear and well-beloved. . .' Quoted in Griffiths, op.cit., p. 255.

Page 178: death of Gloucester. Seward, op.cit., p. 246; Norwich, op.cit., p. 254.

Page 179–80: Charles VII's administration. Perroy, op.cit., p. 297–304; Seward, op.cit., p. 247.

Page 180: English evacuation of Maine and attack on Fougères. Perroy, op.cit., p. 316–7; Seward, op.cit., p. 248.

Page 180: 'Sir Francis. . .' Thompson, op.cit., p. 327.

Page 181: plot to support the younger brother of the Duke of Brittany. Griffiths, op.cit., p. 511.

Page 181: French victories of 1449. Neillands, op.cit., p. 281–2; Seward, op.cit., p. 248–9.

Pages 184–5: 'Within a year they were to pay. . .' Thompson, op.cit., p. 334–5.

Page 185: mutiny of Kyriel's troops. Seward, op.cit., p. 249.

Page 186: Battle of Formigny. Seward, op.cit., p. 250–1; Neillands, op.cit., p. 282–3.

Page 187: release of Talbot. Neillands, p. 283; Seward, op.cit., p. 260.

Page 187: 'The town received. . .' Thompson op.cit., p. 336.

Page 187: refugees return from France. Wolffe, op.cit., p. 211–12.

Page 188–9: Cade rebellion. Seward, op.cit., p. 255–6; Norwich, op.cit., p. 257–60.

Pages 189–90: charges against Suffolk and his death. Seward, op.cit., p. 255; Norwich, op.cit., p. 256.

Page 190: French artillery. Seward, op.cit., p. 258.

Page 190: Gironde fleet. Griffiths, op.cit., p. 259.

Page 194: secret envoys from Bordeaux. Seward, op.cit., p. 257.

Page 194: 'It is our intention. . .' Quoted in Griffiths, op.cit., p. 531.

Pages 194–8: Battle of Castillon. Seward, op.cit., p. 259–62. Neillands, op.cit., p. 287.

Page 198: surrender of Bordeaux. Neillands, op.cit., p. 288; Seward, op.cit., p. 262.

Page 198: madness of Henry VI. Norwich, op.cit., p. 263.

Notes to Epilogue

Pages 200–1: Thomas Basin description. Quoted by Robert Boutrouche in *The Devastation of Rural Areas during the Hundred Years War and the Agricultural Recovery of France* in P.S. Lewis (Ed.) *The Recovery of France in the Fifteenth Century* Macmillan (London) 1971 p. 26–7.

Page 201: John Fortescue quotation. Ibid.

Page 201: 'I have chased the English out of France...' Quoted by Neillands, op.cit., p. 290.

Page 201: Terms of the Treaty of Picquigny. Seward, op.cit., p. 264.

Page 202: Treaty of Picquigny the true end of the war? Neillands, op.cit., p. 291.

Page 202: English claims to the French throne lasting until 1802. Seward, op.cit., p. 264.

Further Reading

The short selection of books listed below represents a small part of the extensive literature on the Hundred Years War – chosen as likely to be of most interest to the general reader.

ALLMAND, CHRISTOPHER. *The Hundred Years War* (Cambridge University Press, Cambridge, 1989)

ALLMAND, CHRISTOPHER. *Henry V* (Yale University Press, New Haven and London, 1997. First published by Methuen, London 1992)

BARBER, RICHARD. *Edward, Prince of Wales and Aquitaine* (Boydell Press, Woodbridge, 1978)

CURRY, ANNE. *The Hundred Years War* (Macmillan, Basingstoke, 1993)

DEVRIES, KELLY. *Joan of Arc, A Military Leader* (Sutton, Stroud, 1999)

EARLE, PETER. *The Life and Times of Henry V* (Weidenfeld & Nicholson, London, 1972)

GRIFFITHS, R.A. *The Reign of King Henry VI* (Sutton, Stroud, 1981)

HIBBERT, CHRISTOPHER. *Agincourt* (Windrush Press, Moreton-in-Marsh, 1996 edition p. 76–79. First published in UK, 1978)

JACOB, YVES. *Bertrand du Guesclin* (Tallandier, Paris, 1992)

LLOYD, ALAN. *The Hundred Years War* (Book Club Associates, London, 1977)

LUCIE-SMITH, EDWARD. *Joan of Arc* (Allen Lane, London, 1976)

McKISACK, MAY. The Fourteenth Century (Oxford University Press, Oxford, 1959)

NEILLANDS, ROBIN. *The Hundred Years War* (Guild, London, 1990)

NORWICH, JOHN JULIUS. *Shakespeare's Kings* (Viking, London, 1999)

PERROY, EDOUARD. *The Hundred Years War* (Eyre & Spottiswoode, London, 1962)

SEWARD, DESMOND. *The Hundred Years War* (Constable, London, 1978)

JONATHAN SUMPTION. *The Hundred Years War*. Vol. 1, *Trial by Battle* (Faber, London, 1990. Paperback version University of Pennsylvania Press, 1999); *The Hundred Years War*. Vol. II, *Trial by Fire* (Faber, London, 1999)

THOMPSON, PETER E. (Ed.) *Contemporary Chronicles of the Hundred Years War* (The Folio Society, London, 1966)

TUCHMAN, BARBARA. *A Distant Mirror* (Macmillan, London, 1979. Also, Papermac, 1995)

WARNER, MARINA. *Joan of Arc* (Vintage, London, 1981)

WOLFFE, BERTRAM. *Henry VI* (Eyre Methuen, London, 1981)

Index

Italic page numbers indicate maps or charts; bold page numbers indicate feature information